The Sacred Flame
Unlocking Spiritual Power
By Lily Cooper

Copyright © Vellaz Publishing 2022

All rights reserved.
No part of this book may be reproduced by any means without written permission from the copyright holder.

Cover image © Vellaz Studio
Review by Armando Vellaz
Graphic design by Amadeu Brumm
Layout by Matheus Costa
All rights reserved to: Vellaz Publishing

Holism

Summary

Prologue 5
Chapter 1 Holistic Healing of Saint Germain 7
Chapter 2 The Sacred Flames and Their Importance in Healing 14
Chapter 3 Energy Cleansing: Preparing the Auric Field 22
Chapter 4 Meditations for Aligning with the Energy of Saint Germain
 31
Chapter 5 Using the Violet Flame to Transmute Negative Energies ... 40
Chapter 6 Healing Emotional and Karmic Wounds 49
Chapter 7 Self-Healing: Applying the Techniques to Yourself 58
Chapter 8 Distance Healing: Theory and Fundamentals 67
Chapter 9 The Power of the Spoken Word and Decrees in Healing ... 76
Chapter 10 The Violet Flame and Physical Body Transformation 85
Chapter 11 Crystals and the Violet Flame 94
Chapter 12 Energy Protection for the Healer 103
Chapter 13 Balancing the Chakras with the Energy of Saint Germain
 113
Chapter 14 Purifying Spaces with the Violet Flame 122
Chapter 15 Healing Relationships with the Violet Flame 129
Chapter 16 Working with Spiritual Guides in Healing 138
Chapter 17 Holistic Healing in Children - 146
Chapter 18 Preparing Crystal Elixirs and the Violet Flame 155
Chapter 19 Healing Through Dreams and Spiritual Connection 164
Chapter 20 Healing Ancestral and Inherited Patterns 173

Chapter 21 Harmonizing Your Relationship with Money and Abundance 182

Chapter 22 Healing Chronic Illnesses with the Violet Flame 191

Chapter 23 Healing Animals with the Violet Flame 200

Chapter 24 Advancing in Global and Planetary Healing 209

Epilogue 219

Prologue

Imagine for a moment that every pain, every blockage, and every repressed emotion you have ever experienced are echoes of energies moving beyond the surface. Now, visualize a portal before you—an invitation to step into a dimension where sacred flames, guided by the transformative power of spirituality, offer the healing you've always longed for but never knew how to reach. This is not just another path to self-discovery but a journey of deep transcendence, where body, mind, and spirit align to touch what is divine within you.

The book you hold in your hands doesn't promise easy answers but something infinitely more powerful: it invites you to explore the unknown, to dive into subtle layers of energy, and to uncover the hidden truths that rest at the foundation of all existence. These pages are a guide that leads your mind beyond logical understanding and plunges it into a vibrant ocean of spiritual revelations. Throughout the reading, you will not only learn the art of energetic healing but also encounter transformative insights about the purpose of your own journey.

Allow yourself to be enveloped by the mysterious aura of the Sacred Flames. They have the power to cleanse not only your physical wounds but also to work on deep spiritual levels, dissolving the karmic ties that often bind the soul. There is one flame in particular, the Violet Flame, with its transmuting power that acts as a divine balm, purifying dense energies and invisible blockages. Imagine the freedom that comes from leaving behind accumulated traumas and the energies that limit your divine potential.

As you turn these pages, you will not remain the same. Each word is crafted to awaken in you the memory that there is far more than what meets the eye. You will be guided through ancient and sacred practices by spiritual masters who understood the essence of being as a dance between the visible and invisible, the material and spiritual. Here, in this book, healing is not just a technique but a profound reconnection with your true essence. Let the knowledge revealed touch your heart and allow a new way of living to blossom.

Breathe deeply and imagine yourself stepping into a space where rays of sacred light illuminate every corner of your soul. This is the invitation this book makes. By embarking on this reading, you are opening a door to levels of consciousness that many have not yet dared to explore. The unknown you are about to uncover is, in truth, a part of you that has always waited to be rediscovered.

You will be called to experience practices that go beyond the rational mind, entering into meditative states that align your energy field with universal forces. Imagine yourself tuning into spiritual frequencies that renew the body, clear the mind, and elevate your soul. What you will find here is a path that not only leads to healing but also to awakening. Allow yourself to feel the power in each page, the energy that touches both the heart and consciousness.

This is the beginning of something greater than you can imagine. You are on the threshold of a profound discovery—and as you move forward, each practice, each meditation, and each flame with which you will connect will open new paths on your journey. This is not merely a book of techniques, but a portal to a living experience of healing and transformation. What you will find are not just answers but truths that resonate with the very frequency of your soul.

The key lies in your decision to open the door and walk through it. The power is already within you; this book is merely the catalyst to awaken it. Allow yourself to dive in without reservations and explore the mysteries that await—a new horizon of healing, peace, and a deep reconnection with the wholeness of your being. The sacred flames await your presence, ready to show you what has always been within your reach: the power to transform and transmute your life into its purest expression.

Chapter 1
Holistic Healing of Saint Germain

Holistic healing, as taught by Saint Germain, emphasizes the interconnectedness of the body, mind, and spirit. It is not just about addressing physical symptoms but understanding that true healing encompasses all aspects of our being. When we are out of balance in any area—emotionally, mentally, or spiritually—it reflects in our physical health. Saint Germain's approach invites us to look beyond the surface and delve into the deeper layers of our energy system to restore harmony.

At the core of Saint Germain's teachings is the idea that energy is the foundation of everything. Our thoughts, emotions, and physical conditions are all expressions of energy vibrating at different frequencies. When our energy is flowing freely and vibrating at a high frequency, we experience health, vitality, and mental clarity. However, when our energy becomes stagnant or is lowered due to negative thoughts, unresolved emotions, or spiritual disconnection, it manifests as illness or emotional imbalance. Understanding this principle is key to unlocking the potential of holistic healing.

A significant aspect of Saint Germain's teachings is the understanding that spiritual energy can be harnessed to promote healing. This energy, often referred to as divine light or universal life force, is available to everyone and can be channeled through various methods, such as meditation, visualization, or the use of sacred flames, especially the Violet Flame, which Saint Germain is famously associated with. The Violet Flame is a transformative spiritual energy that has the power to transmute lower vibrations into higher ones, clearing away negativity and facilitating deep healing on all levels.

Raising our energetic vibration is a fundamental part of this healing process. When we consciously work to elevate our frequency, we align ourselves with higher dimensions of spiritual energy, making it easier for healing to occur. This is where practices such as meditation, breathwork, and focusing on positive thoughts come into play. By raising our vibration, we not only heal ourselves but also contribute to the healing of the collective, as we become more aligned with the universal flow of love and light.

Saint Germain teaches that healing is not just an individual process, but one that is deeply connected to our spiritual evolution. When we heal ourselves, we are clearing the blocks that prevent us from fully expressing our divine nature. This process of clearing allows us to experience higher states of consciousness, where we can connect with our soul's purpose and live more authentically. Therefore, holistic healing is not just about alleviating physical symptoms but is also a pathway to spiritual awakening and personal transformation.

A key component in Saint Germain's approach to holistic healing is the recognition that the mind plays a powerful role in shaping our health. Our thoughts, whether positive or negative, influence our energetic vibration and thus our physical state. Negative thinking, fear, or unresolved emotional issues create blockages in our energy field, which can eventually manifest as physical ailments. Therefore, part of the healing process involves learning to master our thoughts and emotions, recognizing the power of the mind to create both illness and wellness.

Learning to harness spiritual energy for healing begins with the understanding that we are not separate from the divine. Each of us carries within a spark of divine light, and when we tap into this inner divinity, we can direct this energy to where it is most needed. This connection to the divine is strengthened through practices such as prayer, meditation, and the use of sacred symbols and decrees. These practices help to align our personal energy field with higher spiritual frequencies, creating a channel through which healing energy can flow.

Another important aspect of Saint Germain's teachings is the role of the soul in the healing journey. Healing is not simply about curing a physical disease, but rather about restoring the soul's harmony with the divine plan. When we experience illness or imbalance, it is often a sign that we have strayed from our soul's true path. By reconnecting with our soul's purpose and aligning with higher spiritual energies, we allow for a deeper level of healing to take place, one that addresses not just the symptoms but the underlying causes of our dis-ease.

Holistic healing as taught by Saint Germain encourages individuals to take responsibility for their own healing. While external support from healers, doctors, or spiritual guides can be beneficial, true healing ultimately comes from within. It is about cultivating a relationship with our own energy, learning to listen to the body's signals, and making the necessary adjustments to bring ourselves back into balance. This self-empowerment is a crucial aspect of holistic healing, as it encourages individuals to become active participants in their own well-being.

In addition to working with personal energy, Saint Germain emphasizes the importance of healing within the broader context of the world. Each individual's healing journey contributes to the healing of the collective. When we clear our own energy field of negativity, we help to raise the vibration of the planet as a whole. This is why Saint Germain's teachings are not just for personal transformation but are also a call to serve as lightworkers, using our healing abilities to assist others and contribute to the greater good.

The holistic healing journey with Saint Germain is one that requires patience, commitment, and a deep willingness to explore the spiritual dimensions of health. It is not a quick fix or a surface-level solution, but a profound transformation that touches every aspect of our being. Through the integration of body, mind, and spirit, we are able to achieve true healing that extends beyond the physical and leads to lasting peace, joy, and spiritual fulfillment. By raising our vibration and learning to work with spiritual energy, we open ourselves to the limitless possibilities of healing and personal evolution.

The journey into holistic healing, as taught by Saint Germain, begins with preparation—aligning oneself as a pure channel for healing energies. This process involves a deep commitment to raising one's vibrational frequency and establishing a connection with the higher realms of spiritual energy. In this context, meditation and energy alignment play crucial roles in preparing the practitioner to receive and channel divine energy effectively.

Meditation is central to holistic healing. Through consistent practice, meditation trains the mind to achieve a state of stillness, which is necessary for tuning into subtle energy fields. In the stillness of meditation, we quiet the mental chatter that often distracts us from connecting with our higher self and spiritual guides. Saint Germain emphasizes that only when the mind is calm and clear can we fully open ourselves to the healing energies that flow from the divine. This state of inner peace allows us to become receptive to the transformative power of spiritual light, which is the foundation of holistic healing.

One of the first steps in meditation is learning to center oneself. This practice involves bringing attention to the present moment and consciously letting go of distractions, worries, or negative emotions that may be clouding the mind. By focusing on the breath or a specific point of light, the practitioner begins to release tension and align with their inner core of peace. Centering not only prepares the individual for deeper meditation but also serves as a daily practice for maintaining emotional and mental balance.

As meditation deepens, the practitioner learns to move beyond mere relaxation into a state of heightened awareness. This heightened awareness allows for the perception of subtle energies that may not be apparent in everyday life. In this expanded state of consciousness, the practitioner can sense the flow of energy within their body and the surrounding environment. This is an essential step in energy alignment, as it helps to identify areas of imbalance or blockage that need attention.

Energy alignment is the process of bringing the practitioner's energetic field into harmony with the higher spiritual vibrations. Saint Germain teaches that our energy centers, or chakras, must be clear and aligned for healing energy to flow freely. When these centers are blocked or misaligned, it becomes difficult to channel spiritual energy effectively, leading to incomplete or ineffective healing. Therefore, part of the preparation involves working with the chakras to ensure they are open, balanced, and functioning properly.

A simple yet powerful meditation for aligning the chakras involves visualizing each energy center as a spinning wheel of light. Starting at the base of the spine with the root chakra, the practitioner visualizes a vibrant red light spinning and growing brighter with each breath. Moving upward, they visualize the sacral chakra as a bright orange light, the solar plexus as yellow, the heart as green, the throat as blue, the third eye as indigo, and the crown as violet or white. As each chakra is visualized, the practitioner breathes deeply, allowing any stagnant energy to be released and replaced with pure, vibrant light.

Another essential aspect of preparation is establishing a connection with Saint Germain and the Violet Flame. The Violet Flame is not just a tool for transmutation but also a means of purification for the practitioner. Before engaging in any healing work, Saint Germain advises invoking the Violet Flame to cleanse one's aura and energy field. This practice ensures that the practitioner is working with clear, high-frequency energy and is not unconsciously carrying any negativity or blockages that could interfere with the healing process.

To invoke the Violet Flame, the practitioner can use a simple decree or affirmation, such as: "I AM a being of Violet Fire, I AM the purity God desires." By repeating this decree while visualizing the Violet Flame surrounding their body, the practitioner invites this spiritual energy to dissolve any lower vibrations, preparing them to serve as a clear and effective channel for healing. The use of decrees, in combination with visualization, is a powerful technique that amplifies the practitioner's ability to work with spiritual energy.

In addition to meditation and energy alignment, Saint Germain's teachings emphasize the importance of setting clear intentions before any healing work. Intention is the guiding force behind the flow of energy. By clearly defining the purpose of the healing—whether it be to clear blockages, restore balance, or promote spiritual awakening—the practitioner directs the energy toward a specific goal. Without a clear intention, the energy may not be as focused or effective. Therefore, taking time before each healing session to reflect on the desired outcome and aligning one's thoughts and emotions with that intention is an essential part of the preparation process.

Another preparatory practice is grounding, which helps to anchor the practitioner's energy into the physical plane. While spiritual healing involves working with higher vibrations, it is important to remain connected to the Earth, ensuring that the energy is effectively integrated into the physical body. Grounding can be achieved through simple visualizations, such as imagining roots extending from the feet into the Earth, or through physical activities like walking barefoot on the ground. This practice stabilizes the practitioner's energy field and prevents feelings of disorientation or fatigue that can sometimes occur after deep spiritual work.

Saint Germain also teaches that proper preparation includes cultivating a state of compassion and unconditional love. Healing energies flow most powerfully when the practitioner is in a heart-centered state. This means letting go of judgment, fear, or personal agenda, and instead opening the heart to the universal flow of love. By entering into a state of pure, loving intention, the practitioner aligns with the highest frequencies of divine light, allowing the healing energies to work through them effortlessly. This heart-centered approach not only benefits the recipient of the healing but also uplifts the practitioner, fostering their own spiritual growth and well-being.

Finally, Saint Germain's holistic healing requires an ongoing commitment to personal growth and self-care. The practitioner must continually work on their own healing and spiritual development to maintain their ability to channel healing energies effectively. This includes regular meditation, energy cleansing, and self-reflection to ensure that their own energy remains balanced and aligned with the higher spiritual frequencies. The more the practitioner clears their own energetic blockages and raises their vibration, the more powerful their healing abilities become.

In conclusion, the preparation for holistic healing according to Saint Germain is a multifaceted process. It involves meditation to still the mind, energy alignment to clear the chakras, invoking the Violet Flame for purification, setting clear intentions, grounding to connect with the Earth, and cultivating a heart-centered state of love and compassion. By engaging in these practices, the practitioner prepares themselves to act as a pure channel for divine healing energies, opening the door to transformative healing for themselves and others. This preparation is not a one-time event but an ongoing journey, one that deepens the practitioner's connection to their own divine essence and the universal flow of spiritual energy.

Chapter 2
The Sacred Flames and Their Importance in Healing

Central to the teachings of Saint Germain is the use of Sacred Flames as spiritual tools for transformation and healing. These flames represent various divine energies, each with its unique purpose, and are powerful allies in holistic healing. Among them, the Violet Flame is perhaps the most well-known and essential in Saint Germain's approach. It serves as a bridge between the physical and spiritual realms, allowing us to transmute lower energies into higher, purer vibrations, facilitating healing at every level of our being—physical, emotional, mental, and spiritual.

The Sacred Flames are not physical in nature but are manifestations of divine energy that can be accessed through spiritual practice, intention, and invocation. Each flame carries a distinct color and frequency, representing different aspects of the divine will. For example, the Blue Flame is associated with divine protection and strength, the Green Flame with healing and balance, the Pink Flame with unconditional love, and the Violet Flame with transmutation and forgiveness. By invoking these flames, we invite their corresponding energies into our lives, creating a direct link to higher realms of consciousness and healing.

The Violet Flame, in particular, plays a fundamental role in the teachings of Saint Germain. It is the Flame of Transmutation, which means it has the power to transform and purify lower frequencies of energy into higher ones. This is essential in the process of healing because many illnesses and emotional disturbances are the result of stagnant, dense energies that have accumulated in the body, mind, or spirit. These energies can stem from negative thoughts, unresolved emotions, past traumas, or even karmic imbalances. The Violet Flame works by dissolving these heavy energies, transforming them into light and freeing the individual from their burden.

One of the most remarkable aspects of the Violet Flame is its ability to transmute negative karma. Karma is often described as the spiritual principle of cause and effect, where actions from the past, whether in this lifetime or previous ones, can influence our current reality. Negative karma can manifest as recurring patterns of illness, emotional distress, or difficult life circumstances. The Violet Flame, when invoked with sincere intent, can dissolve the karmic energies that keep these patterns in place, allowing for deep healing and the release of old cycles. This doesn't negate personal responsibility, but it provides an opportunity to accelerate healing by addressing the energetic roots of our issues.

To invoke the Violet Flame, one must engage in a simple yet profound spiritual practice. Visualization plays a key role in this process, as it helps to focus the mind and energy. The practitioner begins by visualizing a brilliant Violet Flame surrounding their body or a specific area in need of healing. They can imagine the flame gently moving through their energy field, dissolving any dark or stagnant energies and transforming them into light. The practice is often accompanied by a decree or affirmation, such as: "I AM a being of Violet Fire, I AM the purity God desires." This affirmation, repeated with focused intention, serves to anchor the Violet Flame into the practitioner's energy field.

While the Violet Flame is a powerful tool for personal healing, it also extends its benefits to others and the broader environment. Saint Germain teaches that we can invoke the Violet Flame on behalf of others, sending healing energy to loved ones or even to the collective consciousness. By visualizing the Violet Flame enveloping a person, place, or situation, we can help to transmute negative energies and bring about positive transformation. This practice is especially beneficial in situations where there is conflict, illness, or emotional distress, as it works to clear the energy field of negativity, making space for healing and resolution.

The Violet Flame also has the unique ability to penetrate deep into the subconscious mind, where many of our limiting beliefs and emotional wounds reside. These subconscious patterns often create energetic blockages that prevent us from fully healing or moving forward in life. Through regular use of the Violet Flame, these hidden patterns can be brought to the surface and transmuted, freeing us from the unconscious programming that has been influencing our health and well-being. This aspect of the Violet Flame makes it an invaluable tool for those on a path of personal growth and spiritual awakening.

Beyond the Violet Flame, other Sacred Flames are equally important in the holistic healing process. The Blue Flame, for instance, is invoked for protection and strength. In healing work, it serves as a shield against negative influences or energies that may try to interfere with the process. By surrounding oneself with the Blue Flame, a practitioner can create a protective barrier, ensuring that the healing energy remains pure and uncontaminated by external forces. This flame is particularly useful for healers, as it protects their energy field while working with others, preventing them from absorbing any of the negative energy they may encounter during a session.

The Green Flame, another vital tool in Saint Germain's teachings, is associated with physical healing and balance. It represents the energy of renewal and restoration, helping to bring the body and mind back into harmony. When working with the Green Flame, the practitioner focuses on restoring balance to the body's systems, whether that involves physical ailments, emotional turbulence, or mental stress. The Green Flame works to heal not just the symptoms of disease but also the underlying energetic causes, promoting long-term health and wellness. By invoking this flame, we align ourselves with the natural healing forces of the universe, allowing our bodies and minds to restore themselves to their optimal state.

The Pink Flame of unconditional love is another powerful energy in the context of holistic healing. Love is the highest frequency in the universe, and when we align with this vibration, it has a profoundly healing effect on our entire being. The Pink Flame is especially useful in emotional healing, as it helps to dissolve feelings of fear, anger, or resentment, replacing them with love, compassion, and forgiveness. This flame can be invoked to heal relationships, soothe emotional wounds, and restore a sense of peace and harmony within the heart. By working with the Pink Flame, we open ourselves to receive and give love more freely, which is a vital component of holistic healing.

The Sacred Flames also work together in harmony. For example, a healing session might begin with the Blue Flame for protection, followed by the Violet Flame for transmutation, and then the Green Flame to restore balance and the Pink Flame to infuse love into the process. Each flame plays its role in creating a holistic healing environment, addressing the different layers of the individual's energy field and ensuring a comprehensive healing experience. By integrating the Sacred Flames into one's spiritual practice, the practitioner taps into the full spectrum of divine energies available for healing and transformation.

Saint Germain's teachings on the Sacred Flames remind us that we are not limited to the physical realm when it comes to healing. We have access to powerful spiritual energies that can assist us in our journey toward health and wholeness. The Sacred Flames are tools for transmuting, healing, and elevating our consciousness, helping us to release what no longer serves us and align with the higher frequencies of love, light, and peace. Through the regular use of these flames, we can experience profound healing not just on a physical level, but also emotionally, mentally, and spiritually, paving the way for a life of greater harmony and alignment with our true divine nature.

The practical application of the Sacred Flames is at the heart of Saint Germain's holistic healing techniques. While the understanding of each flame and its spiritual properties is foundational, the next crucial step is learning how to effectively invoke and direct these energies for personal and collective healing. This process is not only an act of spiritual alignment but also a conscious collaboration with the divine, where the practitioner acts as a conduit for these powerful forces to bring about transformation and restoration.

To begin applying the Sacred Flames, it's essential to develop a daily practice of invocation. Invocation is more than simply calling upon the flames; it's a form of spiritual command, where the practitioner, through their divine connection, directs the energy of the flame toward a specific purpose or area in need of healing. The act of invoking the flames can be done through decrees, affirmations, visualization, or even focused meditation. The key is to approach the process with clarity, sincerity, and intention.

One of the most accessible ways to begin invoking the Sacred Flames is through decrees. A decree is a spoken affirmation that channels the energy of the flame. For instance, to invoke the Violet Flame, one might say: "I AM a being of Violet Fire, I AM the purity God desires." This simple yet potent decree calls upon the transforming power of the Violet Flame to cleanse and purify the individual's energy field. Decrees should be repeated with conviction and focus, allowing the practitioner to embody the flame's energy with each repetition. The more decrees are practiced, the stronger the connection to the flame becomes, amplifying its healing effects.

Another powerful technique for invoking the flames is through visualization. Visualization helps to focus the mind and direct the flame's energy where it is needed. For example, when working with the Violet Flame for healing, the practitioner may close their eyes and imagine a vibrant violet light engulfing their entire body. They may visualize this flame moving through their energy field, dissolving dark or dense areas of blocked energy. With each breath, the flame grows brighter and more intense, transmuting all negativity into pure, radiant light. This visual process activates the flame on an energetic level, allowing it to work deeply within the individual's energy body.

When using the Sacred Flames for specific healing purposes, it's important to focus on particular areas of the body, mind, or emotions that require attention. For instance, someone dealing with chronic pain might focus the Green Flame of healing and balance on the area where the discomfort resides. In this case, the practitioner can visualize the Green Flame penetrating the area of pain, bringing in divine energy to restore harmony and balance to the cells and tissues. Alongside this, decrees such as, "I AM the healing light of the Green Flame, restoring perfect health in this body," can be repeated to direct the flame's energy with precision.

For emotional healing, the Pink Flame of unconditional love is especially powerful. Emotional wounds, such as those caused by grief, trauma, or broken relationships, create energetic imbalances that can affect both the mind and body. To heal these wounds, the practitioner invokes the Pink Flame by visualizing a soft, soothing pink light filling the heart center, dissolving any lingering pain, resentment, or fear. The practitioner can use affirmations like, "I AM filled with the love and compassion of the Pink Flame," allowing this gentle energy to replace negative emotions with peace, love, and forgiveness.

The Sacred Flames are not only effective for self-healing but can also be used to heal others. When healing someone else, it's important to approach the process with humility and respect, understanding that the practitioner is merely a vessel for the divine energies and not the source of healing themselves. To invoke the flames on behalf of another, the practitioner can visualize the person surrounded by the chosen flame, whether it be the Violet Flame for transmutation, the Green Flame for physical healing, or the Pink Flame for emotional support. The energy is directed through intention and visualization, and decrees can be spoken to strengthen the connection to the flame.

An important part of this process is the practitioner's awareness of their own energy field. Before engaging in healing work, whether for oneself or another, it's crucial to cleanse and purify one's own energy. This can be done by invoking the Violet Flame to transmute any lower energies, ensuring that the practitioner is a clear and pure channel for the divine light. Additionally, invoking the Blue Flame for protection creates an energetic shield that prevents any negative energies from being absorbed during the healing process. This step is vital, especially when working with others, as it protects both the practitioner and the recipient from energy contamination or depletion.

Practical exercises for working with the flames can include regular meditation and ritualistic invocations. For instance, a morning ritual may consist of calling upon the Blue Flame for protection as one begins the day, invoking the Violet Flame to clear any residual negativity from the night, and using the Green Flame to set a healing intention for the body and mind. As the practitioner moves through these invocations, they cultivate a daily habit of aligning with these divine energies, which enhances their capacity for healing and spiritual growth.

Visualization exercises can be adapted for specific healing purposes. For example, when using the Violet Flame to heal a relationship, the practitioner may visualize the flame enveloping both themselves and the other person, transmuting any discord, misunderstandings, or negative emotions that exist between them. As the flame works, the practitioner can visualize the relationship being restored to a state of harmony and peace, with both parties surrounded by a glowing violet light. This practice can be further amplified by repeating decrees focused on healing and reconciliation, such as, "I AM the Violet Flame, restoring peace and understanding in this relationship."

In addition to personal and relational healing, the Sacred Flames can be used to cleanse and heal spaces. Physical environments, like homes or workplaces, often accumulate stagnant or negative energy over time, which can impact the well-being of those who inhabit them. By invoking the Sacred Flames—especially the Violet Flame—the practitioner can purify these spaces, creating an environment that supports healing, creativity, and peace. A simple practice involves visualizing the Violet Flame sweeping through the room, cleansing every corner and transmuting any lower vibrations into light. This can be reinforced with decrees like, "I AM the Violet Flame, purifying and transforming this space into a sanctuary of peace."

As the practitioner becomes more skilled in working with the Sacred Flames, they may also incorporate other spiritual tools, such as crystals or sacred geometry, to enhance the healing process. Crystals that resonate with the energies of the flames, like amethyst for the Violet Flame or rose quartz for the Pink Flame, can be placed on the body or in the environment to amplify the healing effects. These crystals serve as conduits for the flame's energy, helping to anchor the divine light more deeply into the physical realm.

Ultimately, the goal of working with the Sacred Flames is not only to bring about healing but also to elevate one's consciousness and align more fully with the divine. As Saint Germain teaches, healing is not just about addressing physical or emotional ailments but is part of a broader process of spiritual awakening and transformation. Through consistent practice with the Sacred Flames, the practitioner learns to attune themselves to higher frequencies of light, dissolving the barriers that separate them from their true divine nature. This process fosters a deeper connection to the divine and helps the practitioner to embody more love, light, and peace in their daily life.

The Sacred Flames, when used with intention, devotion, and practice, become powerful allies on the path to wholeness. Whether invoked for personal healing, to assist others, or to cleanse spaces, these divine energies have the power to transform and uplift every aspect of life. By integrating the flames into their spiritual practice, the practitioner not only facilitates healing but also deepens their connection to the divine and their capacity to serve as a channel for love and light in the world. Through the Sacred Flames, we are reminded of our infinite potential to heal, transform, and evolve.

Chapter 3
Energy Cleansing: Preparing the Auric Field

The auric field, often described as the energy field that surrounds the physical body, plays a crucial role in our overall health and well-being. According to Saint Germain's teachings, this field acts as a protective barrier, a reservoir of personal energy, and a reflection of our physical, emotional, and spiritual state. When the aura is clear and balanced, it supports vitality, emotional stability, and spiritual clarity. However, just like our physical body, the auric field can become cluttered with external energies, emotional residues, and even thought forms that disrupt the flow of life force, leading to imbalance and, eventually, illness.

Cleansing the auric field is essential to maintaining both spiritual and physical health. The aura can be affected by a variety of external influences, including interactions with other people, environmental energies, and even the collective consciousness. Negative emotions such as anger, fear, or anxiety—whether our own or absorbed from others—can create disturbances in the aura. Additionally, certain environments, like busy cities or stressful workplaces, may carry chaotic or stagnant energy that latches onto the aura, creating a sense of heaviness or fatigue. Over time, if left uncleansed, these energies can lead to emotional distress, mental fog, or physical ailments.

The first step in understanding how to cleanse the auric field is recognizing its structure and function. The aura is composed of several layers, each corresponding to different aspects of our being. These layers include the physical, emotional, mental, and spiritual bodies. The physical body is the most immediate and dense, while the outer layers, such as the emotional and mental bodies, are more subtle but equally significant. Each layer interacts with the others, meaning that disturbances in one area can ripple through the entire energy field. For instance, unresolved emotions can manifest as physical pain or illness, while negative thoughts can weigh down the emotional body, affecting our overall mood and resilience.

One of the most effective ways to maintain a healthy auric field is through regular energy cleansing. Energy cleansing practices help to remove accumulated negative or stagnant energy from the aura, restoring its natural vibrancy and flow. Saint Germain emphasizes that energy cleansing is not just a reactive measure when things go wrong, but a proactive and necessary practice for anyone committed to spiritual growth and holistic healing. By keeping the aura clear, we can ensure that our energy remains aligned with higher spiritual frequencies, allowing us to access greater clarity, intuition, and strength.

Cleansing the auric field begins with awareness. It's important to regularly check in with your energy field and notice any signs of imbalance. These signs can be subtle, such as feeling unusually fatigued or emotionally heavy without a clear reason, or more obvious, like experiencing physical symptoms or chronic stress. Taking time each day to meditate and tune into your body's sensations and emotional state can help you detect these imbalances early. Once you become aware of disruptions in your aura, you can then take steps to cleanse and restore its harmony.

A simple yet powerful method for auric cleansing is through the use of visualization. This practice involves imagining yourself surrounded by a bright, radiant light that sweeps through your energy field, dissolving any lower vibrations or energetic debris. You can begin by sitting in a comfortable position, closing your eyes, and taking deep, cleansing breaths. As you breathe in, imagine pure, white light entering through the crown of your head, filling your entire body with healing energy. As you exhale, visualize this light expanding outward, pushing away any dark or heavy energy from your aura.

For a more focused approach, the Violet Flame can be invoked to cleanse the auric field. The Violet Flame is particularly effective in transmuting negative energies, making it an ideal tool for clearing the aura. To use the Violet Flame, simply visualize a violet light surrounding your body, starting from your feet and moving upward, engulfing your entire aura in its transformative energy. Imagine the flame gently dissolving any blocks or impurities in your energy field, leaving behind only pure, vibrant light. You can reinforce this visualization by repeating a decree, such as, "I AM a being of Violet Fire, I AM the purity God desires." This combination of visualization and decree helps to activate the Violet Flame's healing power, ensuring a thorough cleansing of the auric field.

Another key method for cleansing the aura involves using the natural elements, particularly water. Water is a powerful conductor of energy and has long been associated with purification and healing. Taking a bath with the intention of cleansing your energy field can be a deeply restorative practice. You can enhance this by adding sea salt or Epsom salts to the water, as salt has the ability to absorb negative energy. As you soak, visualize the water drawing out any impurities from your aura, washing them away. As you drain the bath, imagine all the negative energy flowing down the drain, leaving you feeling refreshed and revitalized.

In addition to salt baths, the use of herbal infusions can also support auric cleansing. Certain herbs, such as sage, lavender, and rosemary, carry high vibrational properties that help to clear and uplift the energy field. Sage, in particular, is known for its ability to dispel negative energy. You can create an herbal bath by steeping these herbs in hot water and then adding the infusion to your bathwater. Alternatively, smudging—burning sage or other sacred herbs and allowing the smoke to surround your body—can be an effective way to cleanse your aura. As the smoke rises, it carries away any stagnant or negative energies from your field, leaving you feeling lighter and more balanced.

Crystals also play a significant role in cleansing and protecting the auric field. Amethyst, known for its connection to the Violet Flame, is particularly effective in transmuting negative energies and purifying the aura. To use crystals for cleansing, simply hold the crystal in your hand or place it on your body during meditation, allowing its energy to harmonize with your own. You can also place crystals around your living space or wear them as jewelry to maintain a constant flow of protective energy. Other crystals, such as black tourmaline and selenite, are known for their grounding and cleansing properties, helping to keep the aura clear and shielded from negative influences.

Grounding techniques are also essential for maintaining a clear auric field. When we are ungrounded, our energy can become scattered, making us more susceptible to absorbing external energies. Grounding involves connecting your energy to the Earth, stabilizing and anchoring yourself in the present moment. One simple grounding exercise is to visualize roots extending from your feet into the Earth, anchoring you firmly to its core. As you breathe, imagine Earth's energy rising through these roots, filling your body and aura with a sense of stability and calm. This grounding practice not only strengthens your energy field but also helps to discharge any excess or unwanted energy.

Another aspect of auric cleansing involves emotional hygiene. Just as we cleanse our physical bodies daily, we must also regularly release emotional and mental toxins. Negative emotions, such as anger, fear, or resentment, can create tears or imbalances in the aura if left unaddressed. It's important to process these emotions in a healthy way, whether through journaling, talking with a trusted friend or therapist, or practicing mindful breathing. By regularly releasing emotional baggage, you help to maintain the integrity and strength of your auric field.

Saint Germain's teachings remind us that cleansing the aura is not a one-time event but a continuous practice. Just as we wouldn't go long periods without bathing our physical body, we must regularly cleanse our auric field to keep our energy vibrant and flowing. Incorporating these practices into your daily routine—whether it's a quick visualization, a morning decree, or a weekly salt bath—ensures that your energy remains aligned, protected, and ready to receive the higher spiritual energies necessary for healing and growth.

By committing to regular energy cleansing, we not only protect ourselves from external influences but also create a clearer channel for divine energy to flow through us. This clear and balanced state allows us to be more receptive to spiritual guidance, experience deeper emotional peace, and maintain physical vitality. Through these practices, we step into a greater awareness of our energetic body and take responsibility for nurturing our holistic health.

One of the most effective tools for auric cleansing is the use of crystals. Crystals act as amplifiers and conduits of spiritual energy, helping to clear and stabilize the auric field. Different crystals resonate with specific frequencies and can be used to target particular aspects of the energy body. For instance, amethyst is closely linked with the transmutational power of the Violet Flame, making it an ideal crystal for clearing and purifying the aura. When using amethyst, simply hold the crystal in your hand or place it on your body during meditation. As you breathe deeply, visualize the amethyst radiating violet light throughout your auric field, dissolving any negative or heavy energies and replacing them with pure, high-frequency vibrations.

Black tourmaline is another powerful crystal for auric protection. Known for its grounding and shielding properties, black tourmaline helps to repel negative energies and create a protective barrier around the aura. To use black tourmaline, you can carry it with you throughout the day, wear it as jewelry, or place it near your workspace or home to ensure a constant flow of protective energy. Combining black tourmaline with selenite, a crystal known for its purifying and cleansing properties, creates a powerful duo for maintaining the auric field. Selenite helps to clear the aura of any residual negative energy while raising the vibration of your energy body, making it an essential tool for daily cleansing.

In addition to crystals, the use of herbal baths is an ancient and highly effective method for auric cleansing. Water, as a natural conductor of energy, has the ability to absorb and release emotional, mental, and spiritual blockages from the auric field. When combined with specific herbs, it becomes a potent medium for purification and healing. Sage, lavender, rosemary, and eucalyptus are some of the most commonly used herbs for energy cleansing. Sage, in particular, is known for its powerful ability to dispel negative energies and restore balance to the energy body.

To create an herbal bath, simply steep the chosen herbs in boiling water for 10-15 minutes, strain the infusion, and add it to your bathwater. As you immerse yourself in the bath, visualize the water surrounding your body with light, gently washing away any energetic debris or negativity. You can enhance this practice by setting an intention for the bath, such as, "I release all that no longer serves me, and I invite light and clarity into my energy field." As you soak, breathe deeply and allow the herbs to do their work, clearing and fortifying your aura. When you're ready to drain the bath, imagine all the negative energy being washed away, leaving you feeling refreshed and restored.

The Violet Flame, as taught by Saint Germain, is one of the most powerful spiritual tools available for auric cleansing. This flame is not only capable of transmuting negative energies but also of raising the overall vibration of the auric field. By regularly invoking the Violet Flame, you can keep your aura clear and aligned with higher spiritual frequencies. To incorporate the Violet Flame into your daily practice, take a few moments each day to visualize the flame surrounding your entire body. Imagine the flame moving through your energy field, transforming any dark or heavy areas into radiant light. As you do this, you can use a decree such as, "I AM a being of Violet Fire, I AM the purity God desires," to reinforce your connection to the Violet Flame and amplify its effects.

Smudging, or the burning of sacred herbs, is another powerful and practical method for auric cleansing. Sage, palo santo, and cedar are commonly used for this purpose, as their smoke carries purifying properties that help to clear the energy field. To perform a smudging ritual, light your chosen herb and allow the smoke to rise. Gently wave the smoke around your body, starting at your feet and moving upward toward your head, making sure to cover the entire auric field. As you do this, focus on releasing any stagnant or negative energies, and visualize the smoke carrying them away. Smudging is especially effective after spending time in crowded or stressful environments or after emotionally challenging experiences.

In addition to smudging, sound can be used to cleanse and balance the auric field. Sound has a vibrational quality that resonates with different frequencies in the body and energy field. Instruments such as singing bowls, tuning forks, and bells produce tones that help to dislodge and clear blocked energy from the aura. When using sound for cleansing, begin by striking the instrument and allowing the sound to wash over your body. Close your eyes and focus on the vibrations as they interact with your energy field. You may feel certain areas of your body respond to the sound, especially if they are holding tension or energetic blockages. As the sound waves pass through your aura, they help to break up stagnant energy, restoring flow and harmony to your energy body.

Grounding practices are equally important for maintaining a strong and clear auric field. When we are ungrounded, our energy can become scattered, making it easier for external influences to affect us. Grounding helps to stabilize the aura and reconnect us to the Earth's energy, providing a solid foundation for our spiritual and energetic health. One simple grounding practice is to walk barefoot on the Earth, allowing your body to connect directly with the natural energy of the planet. As you walk, visualize roots extending from your feet deep into the Earth, anchoring your energy and drawing in the Earth's nourishing vibrations. This practice not only grounds the energy body but also helps to release excess or chaotic energies that may have accumulated in the aura.

For those who prefer a more focused grounding meditation, you can sit in a comfortable position and visualize a column of light extending from the base of your spine down into the Earth's core. As you breathe deeply, imagine the Earth's energy rising up through this column, filling your body with stability and strength. This grounding energy not only fortifies your physical body but also strengthens the auric field, creating a protective barrier that shields you from external disruptions.

Another effective method for maintaining the clarity of your auric field is through the use of energetic boundaries. Setting clear energetic boundaries helps to prevent the absorption of unwanted energies from other people or environments. This can be particularly important for those who are highly sensitive or empathic, as they tend to pick up on the emotions and energies of others more easily. To set energetic boundaries, begin by visualizing a protective shield of light around your body. This shield can be any color that resonates with you, though many people find white or gold to be especially effective. As you visualize this shield, affirm that it serves to protect your energy while allowing in only love and light. This practice can be reinforced with a decree such as, "I AM surrounded by divine light, and I am protected from all that does not serve my highest good."

For more intensive cleansing, rituals involving the Violet Flame can be extended to the spaces you inhabit, such as your home or workspace. Just as your auric field can accumulate negative energies, so can the spaces where you spend time. To cleanse a space, begin by invoking the Violet Flame and visualizing it filling the room, moving through walls, floors, ceilings, and all objects within the space. As the Violet Flame sweeps through, imagine it transmuting any lingering negative energies and replacing them with pure, high-frequency light. You can follow this with a smudging ritual or the ringing of a bell to further purify the space and anchor the cleansing process.

As you integrate these cleansing practices into your daily routine, you will likely notice a shift in your energy and overall sense of well-being. Your aura will feel lighter, more vibrant, and more resilient to external influences. This increased clarity in your auric field not only supports physical health but also enhances your emotional and spiritual life, making it easier to connect with your higher self, spiritual guides, and the divine energies that surround you.

By regularly cleansing and maintaining your auric field, you take an active role in protecting and nurturing your energy, creating a foundation for deep healing and personal transformation. Whether through crystals, herbal baths, the Violet Flame, or grounding exercises, the tools for auric cleansing are diverse and adaptable to your unique needs. Through these practices, you can ensure that your energy remains aligned, balanced, and open to the flow of divine light and love.

Chapter 4
Meditations for Aligning with the Energy of Saint Germain

Meditation is a cornerstone of Saint Germain's teachings on holistic healing. It serves as a gateway to higher states of consciousness and a means of aligning oneself with divine energy. Through meditation, we can tap into the healing frequencies that flow from Saint Germain, opening ourselves to receive spiritual guidance and energetic attunement. Meditation also provides the foundation for becoming a clear channel through which the energies of the Sacred Flames, especially the Violet Flame, can flow.

Saint Germain teaches that the process of healing begins with the inner alignment of the mind, body, and spirit. This alignment is facilitated through meditative practices that bring the practitioner into a state of peace, centeredness, and receptivity. When the mind is still and the heart is open, the higher energies of the spiritual realms can flow more freely into our consciousness, initiating profound healing at every level of our being.

One of the primary objectives of meditation in this context is to raise the vibrational frequency of the practitioner. In Saint Germain's teachings, it is emphasized that the higher our frequency, the more aligned we are with divine energies and the more effective our healing work becomes. As we meditate, we begin to shift our awareness from the dense, physical realm to the subtler spiritual realms, where healing energies such as the Violet Flame exist in abundance.

A simple but powerful meditation to connect with Saint Germain involves focusing on the Violet Flame. Begin by sitting in a comfortable position, with your spine straight and your hands resting gently on your lap. Close your eyes and take several deep, cleansing breaths, allowing your body to relax completely. As you breathe, imagine a soft violet light beginning to form above your head. This light represents the energy of the Violet Flame, which Saint Germain oversees. With each breath, allow the violet light to grow brighter and more radiant, enveloping your entire body.

As the Violet Flame surrounds you, visualize it entering your energy field, moving through your chakras, and dissolving any negative or stagnant energy that may be present. You can imagine the flame gently transmuting any fear, anger, or tension into light, leaving your body and mind feeling clear and at peace. Continue to focus on the Violet Flame for several minutes, allowing it to work on all levels of your being. If your mind begins to wander, gently bring your focus back to the sensation of the flame's energy moving through you.

While meditating, it can also be helpful to use a decree to amplify your connection to the energy of Saint Germain. A common decree associated with the Violet Flame is: "I AM a being of Violet Fire, I AM the purity God desires." As you repeat this decree silently or aloud, feel the power of the words aligning you with the higher frequencies of the Violet Flame. The repetition of decrees acts like a mantra, helping to focus the mind and draw in the specific energies you are invoking.

Another meditation that deepens the connection with Saint Germain focuses on the heart center. The heart is a powerful gateway for spiritual energy, and by focusing on this area, we can strengthen our connection to divine love and healing. To begin this meditation, sit comfortably and close your eyes. Place your hands gently over your heart, feeling the warmth and energy of this area. As you breathe deeply, visualize a glowing violet light in the center of your chest. With each breath, see this light expanding, filling your heart with the energy of love, compassion, and forgiveness.

As the violet light continues to grow, imagine it radiating outward, filling your entire body and energy field with its healing presence. Feel the light dissolving any emotional wounds or blockages that may be present, particularly those related to feelings of unworthiness, resentment, or fear. As the light clears these blockages, allow a sense of peace and calm to settle into your heart. This practice not only strengthens your connection to the energy of Saint Germain but also helps to open and heal the heart center, which is essential for holistic healing.

In addition to visualization and decrees, focusing on the breath is an important aspect of meditation in Saint Germain's teachings. Conscious breathing helps to anchor spiritual energy into the physical body, bringing the practitioner into a state of alignment and presence. A simple breathing technique that can be used during meditation is the "4-7-8" breath. To practice this, inhale through your nose for a count of four, hold the breath for a count of seven, and then exhale slowly through your mouth for a count of eight. This breathing pattern helps to calm the mind and nervous system, making it easier to enter a meditative state and receive spiritual energy.

For those who are just beginning their meditation practice, it can be helpful to start with shorter sessions, gradually increasing the length as you become more comfortable. Even just five to ten minutes of meditation each day can make a significant difference in your ability to connect with the energy of Saint Germain and the Violet Flame. Over time, as your practice deepens, you will likely find that you are able to meditate for longer periods, experiencing a greater sense of peace and alignment with the higher energies.

Meditation also opens the practitioner to receive spiritual guidance. Saint Germain's teachings emphasize that during meditation, we can communicate with our higher self, spirit guides, and angels, who can offer insight, healing, and support on our journey. As you meditate, you may begin to receive intuitive impressions, visions, or messages from the spiritual realm. These may come in the form of symbols, images, or feelings. It's important to remain open and receptive, trusting that the guidance you receive is for your highest good. After meditation, take a few moments to reflect on any insights or messages that may have come through, and consider keeping a journal to document your experiences.

Another key aspect of meditation with Saint Germain is the practice of gratitude. Gratitude is a high-vibrational state that aligns us with the divine and opens the flow of healing energy. At the end of each meditation session, take a moment to express gratitude for the healing and guidance you have received. This can be done silently in your heart or spoken aloud. By cultivating gratitude, you strengthen your connection to the energy of Saint Germain and the spiritual support available to you.

Meditation not only supports personal healing but also prepares the practitioner to offer healing to others. By consistently aligning with the higher energies through meditation, you become a more effective channel for the Violet Flame and other Sacred Flames when working with others. Whether you are offering healing through touch, energy work, or prayer, meditation helps to purify and align your energy field, ensuring that you can hold and transmit the highest frequencies of light. This preparation is essential for anyone who wishes to engage in healing work, whether professionally or in service to friends, family, or the collective.

Through regular meditation, the practitioner not only strengthens their connection to Saint Germain and the Violet Flame but also experiences a deepening of their spiritual path. Meditation fosters a sense of inner peace, clarity, and resilience, which are essential qualities for navigating the challenges of daily life. As the practitioner continues to meditate, they may notice an increased sense of purpose and direction, as well as a greater ability to manifest their desires and intentions with ease. These benefits are the result of consistently aligning with the higher frequencies of divine energy through meditation.

Meditation is a powerful tool for aligning with the energy of Saint Germain and the healing forces of the universe. Through visualization, decrees, conscious breathing, and heart-centered practices, the practitioner opens themselves to receive divine energy, facilitating profound healing on all levels. As this connection deepens, the practitioner becomes a clearer channel for the Sacred Flames, embodying the love, light, and wisdom that are essential for holistic healing.

The first meditation focuses on visualizing the complete integration of the Sacred Flames within the practitioner's energy field. This advanced technique involves calling forth multiple Sacred Flames in succession, allowing each to flow through the body and aura to address specific healing needs. Begin by sitting comfortably in a quiet place where you will not be disturbed. Close your eyes and take a few deep breaths, allowing yourself to relax fully. As you breathe, focus on clearing your mind and releasing any distractions.

Start by invoking the Violet Flame, the energy of transmutation. Visualize a brilliant violet light descending from above and surrounding your body. As this light envelops you, imagine it gently moving through each layer of your aura, dissolving any negative or stagnant energies. Feel the warmth and intensity of the flame as it clears away all that no longer serves you, creating space for new, higher frequencies to enter. As you breathe deeply, repeat the decree: "I AM a being of Violet Fire, I AM the purity God desires." Allow yourself to fully experience the sensation of this flame transforming your energy.

Once you feel the Violet Flame has done its work, shift your focus to the Blue Flame, which represents divine protection, strength, and will. Visualize a deep, sapphire blue light surrounding you, infusing your energy field with a sense of security and strength. Feel this protective energy creating a powerful shield around your aura, repelling any negative influences or energies that might try to interfere with your healing. As the Blue Flame moves through your body, repeat the decree: "I AM the Blue Flame of God's protection and strength, safeguarding me in all ways." Allow the energy to ground and fortify you, giving you a strong foundation for the rest of the meditation.

Next, call upon the Pink Flame, which represents unconditional love and compassion. Visualize a soft, glowing pink light emanating from your heart center, expanding outward to fill your entire energy field. As this light moves through you, feel it dissolving any emotional blockages, fears, or resentments, replacing them with love, compassion, and forgiveness. The Pink Flame works to heal emotional wounds and open the heart to deeper levels of connection with the divine. As you breathe, repeat the decree: "I AM filled with the unconditional love of the Pink Flame, healing all wounds and opening my heart to divine love."

Finally, bring in the Green Flame, the energy of healing and balance. Visualize a bright emerald green light flowing into your body, moving through your physical cells, organs, and tissues. As the Green Flame works, imagine it restoring balance and harmony to every part of your being. Focus on any areas of the body that need healing, allowing the Green Flame to infuse those areas with its restorative energy. As you breathe, repeat the decree: "I AM the healing light of the Green Flame, restoring perfect health and balance in my body." Feel a deep sense of wholeness and renewal as the Green Flame completes its work.

To end this meditation, visualize all the Sacred Flames—the Violet, Blue, Pink, and Green Flames—working together in harmony, surrounding your body and energy field. Imagine them merging into a radiant rainbow of light that elevates your entire being to a higher state of consciousness. As you breathe, allow yourself to absorb the frequencies of these divine energies, knowing that you are now aligned with the highest vibrations of love, healing, and protection. Sit quietly for a few more moments, allowing the energy to settle and integrate fully into your system.

Another powerful meditation for deepening your connection with Saint Germain and the Violet Flame is the practice of "Third Eye Activation." This meditation focuses on opening the third eye, or the sixth chakra, located in the center of the forehead. The third eye is the seat of intuition, insight, and spiritual vision, and activating it allows for clearer communication with higher realms and deeper access to spiritual guidance.

To begin, sit comfortably and close your eyes. Take a few deep breaths, centering yourself and relaxing your body. Bring your attention to the area between your eyebrows, where the third eye is located. Visualize a small, glowing indigo or violet light in this area. With each breath, imagine this light becoming brighter and more focused, expanding outward to fill your entire forehead. As you focus on the third eye, you may feel a subtle tingling or warmth in this area, indicating that the energy is beginning to flow.

As the light in your third eye grows stronger, invite the energy of Saint Germain to assist in the activation of this center. Visualize Saint Germain standing before you, holding a radiant Violet Flame in his hands. He places this flame gently on your third eye, infusing it with the transformative power of the Violet Flame. As the flame merges with your third eye, imagine it dissolving any blockages or obstacles that may be preventing you from accessing your intuition or spiritual vision.

As you continue to breathe deeply, repeat the decree: "I AM the Violet Flame, opening my third eye to divine insight and spiritual vision." With each repetition, feel the energy of the Violet Flame working to clear and open your third eye, allowing you to see beyond the physical realm and into the spiritual dimensions. You may begin to receive impressions, images, or feelings as your third eye becomes more active. Trust whatever comes through, knowing that it is part of your spiritual growth and awakening.

Spend several minutes focusing on the third eye and allowing the energy of Saint Germain and the Violet Flame to work. When you feel ready, slowly bring your awareness back to your body, taking a few deep breaths to ground yourself. As you open your eyes, take a moment to reflect on any insights or intuitive messages you received during the meditation. Over time, as you practice this meditation regularly, you will find that your third eye becomes more attuned to spiritual energies, allowing you to access deeper levels of awareness and guidance.

A final meditation for deepening your connection to Saint Germain involves working with the breath to attune to the rhythm of divine energy. This breathwork meditation is known as the "Breath of Light" and focuses on using the breath as a tool for aligning with higher frequencies of spiritual energy.

To begin, sit comfortably with your eyes closed and your hands resting on your knees. Take a few deep breaths, allowing your body to relax and your mind to settle. As you inhale, visualize a stream of golden or violet light entering through the crown of your head, filling your lungs and entire body with light. As you exhale, imagine this light expanding outward, filling your aura with its radiant energy. Continue breathing in this way, with each inhale drawing in more light, and each exhale allowing the light to spread throughout your energy field.

As you focus on the breath, imagine that you are breathing in divine energy from the higher realms. With each breath, you become more aligned with the rhythm of the universe, allowing the energy of Saint Germain to flow through you effortlessly. You can silently repeat the affirmation, "With each breath, I align with the divine energy of Saint Germain and the Violet Flame." This repetition helps to focus your mind and deepen your connection with the energy.

As you continue the Breath of Light meditation, you may begin to feel a sense of expansion, as though your energy is merging with the higher realms. This sensation of expansion indicates that you are attuning to the flow of divine energy, allowing it to move freely through your body and energy field. Spend several minutes in this state of alignment, breathing in light and exhaling love, peace, and healing energy.

When you are ready to conclude the meditation, slowly bring your awareness back to your physical body. Take a few deep breaths to ground yourself, and gently open your eyes. As you come out of the meditation, you may notice a sense of lightness, clarity, and connection to the divine. The Breath of Light meditation helps to maintain this connection throughout the day, allowing you to carry the energy of Saint Germain and the Violet Flame with you wherever you go.

These advanced meditations provide powerful tools for deepening your connection to Saint Germain and accessing the healing energies of the Violet Flame. Through regular practice, you will experience greater alignment with divine energy, enhanced spiritual insight, and a deeper sense of peace and healing in all aspects of your life. As your connection with these higher energies strengthens, you become a clearer channel for healing, both for yourself and for others.

Chapter 5
Using the Violet Flame to Transmute Negative Energies

The Violet Flame, central to the teachings of Saint Germain, is one of the most powerful spiritual tools for transmuting negative energies. It is an alchemical energy that can transform lower vibrations, such as fear, anger, and resentment, into higher frequencies of love, peace, and compassion.

Negative energies can accumulate in our physical, emotional, mental, and spiritual bodies through various means—our thoughts, emotions, interactions with others, and even past karmic debts. These energies create blockages in our energy field, which can manifest as physical illness, emotional distress, or mental confusion. When left unresolved, these blockages not only affect our well-being but can also impede our spiritual growth. The Violet Flame works by transmuting these negative energies at their root, clearing the blockages and restoring the natural flow of energy within and around us.

The first step in working with the Violet Flame is learning how to identify where these blockages or negative energies are located in your body or energy field. Blockages often manifest as physical sensations, such as tension or pain in specific areas of the body. On an emotional level, they can appear as feelings of heaviness, anxiety, or unresolved anger. Mentally, blockages may show up as persistent negative thoughts or limiting beliefs. It is important to tune into your body and energy field regularly to become aware of where these blockages exist.

To begin, take a few moments to sit quietly and bring your awareness to your body. Close your eyes and breathe deeply, allowing yourself to relax. As you scan your body from head to toe, notice any areas where you feel tension, discomfort, or heaviness. These areas are often where energy blockages are present. Pay attention to any emotional or mental patterns that arise during this process—repeated thoughts, memories, or emotions that may indicate unresolved issues. Once you have identified these areas, you are ready to invoke the Violet Flame.

The Violet Flame is called forth through the power of intention, visualization, and spoken decrees. To invoke the flame, begin by visualizing a radiant violet light descending from above and surrounding your entire body. This violet light is the transformative energy of the Violet Flame, and it works by raising the vibration of any negative or stagnant energy it comes into contact with. As you visualize the violet light, focus on the areas of your body or energy field where you identified blockages or discomfort. Imagine the Violet Flame moving through these areas, dissolving and transmuting the negative energy.

As the flame works, you can amplify its effect by repeating a decree. One of the most common decrees for invoking the Violet Flame is: "I AM a being of Violet Fire, I AM the purity God desires." Repeat this decree several times, either silently or aloud, while continuing to visualize the Violet Flame working through your body. Each repetition strengthens the connection to the flame and accelerates the process of transmutation. Feel the energy in your body becoming lighter and more fluid as the blockages are cleared away.

While working with the Violet Flame, it is important to maintain a state of openness and receptivity. The Violet Flame is an intelligent energy that knows exactly where it needs to go and what needs to be healed. Trust in its ability to reach the deepest layers of your being and transmute the energies that are ready to be released. If emotions arise during the process—whether it's sadness, anger, or even joy—allow them to flow freely. These emotions are part of the release and healing process, and by letting them surface, you are allowing the flame to do its work.

For deeper transmutation work, you can also focus on specific aspects of your life where negative patterns or energies have persisted. For example, if you find yourself repeating the same negative behaviors or encountering recurring challenges, this may indicate a deeper karmic pattern that needs to be addressed. The Violet Flame can dissolve these karmic imprints, freeing you from the cycle of negativity and allowing you to move forward with greater clarity and purpose.

One practice for addressing these deeper patterns is to focus on the root cause of the issue, rather than the symptoms. For instance, if you are dealing with a recurring emotional pattern, such as anger or fear, ask yourself what the underlying cause might be. Is it tied to a specific event, relationship, or belief system? Once you have identified the root, visualize the Violet Flame working directly on this aspect of your life. Imagine it dissolving not only the surface symptoms but the core energy that is driving the pattern. Repeat the decree, "I AM the Violet Flame, transmuting all that no longer serves me," while holding the visualization. This process helps to clear the issue at its source, allowing for lasting transformation.

In addition to personal healing, the Violet Flame can also be used to transmute negative energies in your environment. Spaces such as homes, workplaces, or even social settings can accumulate dense or stagnant energies over time, particularly in areas where there has been conflict, illness, or prolonged stress. The Violet Flame is an excellent tool for clearing and uplifting these spaces, restoring harmony and balance.

To use the Violet Flame for space clearing, begin by visualizing a large column of violet light descending into the space you wish to cleanse. Imagine the flame sweeping through every corner of the room, purifying the air, walls, and objects. You can visualize the flame moving through areas where the energy feels particularly heavy or stagnant, dissolving the negative vibrations and filling the space with light. You can also walk through the space while repeating the decree: "I AM the Violet Flame, purifying this space with divine light." As you do this, imagine the energy of the space being lifted and transformed.

One of the most profound applications of the Violet Flame is in the transmutation of collective energies. As we move through our daily lives, we are constantly interacting with the collective consciousness, which includes not only the energies of those around us but also the broader energies of society. These collective energies often carry vibrations of fear, anger, and division, which can affect our personal energy field if we are not vigilant. By working with the Violet Flame, we can transmute these collective energies, contributing to the healing and uplifting of the world around us.

To transmute collective energies, begin by invoking the Violet Flame in your own energy field, allowing it to purify and protect you. Once you feel centered and aligned with the flame, expand your visualization outward, imagining the flame spreading across your community, city, or even the entire planet. See the Violet Flame moving through the hearts and minds of all people, dissolving fear, hatred, and separation, and replacing them with love, unity, and compassion. As you hold this vision, repeat the decree: "I AM the Violet Flame, transmuting all negative energies on Earth and restoring divine harmony." This practice not only helps to protect your own energy but also serves as a powerful act of service to the world.

The Violet Flame's ability to transmute negative energies extends beyond the physical realm to the mental and emotional bodies. Negative thought patterns, such as self-doubt, criticism, or fear, can create energetic blockages that impede our spiritual growth and manifest as challenges in our lives. By regularly working with the Violet Flame, we can dissolve these limiting thought forms and replace them with thoughts aligned with love, empowerment, and divine purpose.

One technique for transmuting mental and emotional energies is to identify a specific thought or emotion that you wish to transform. For example, if you find yourself constantly thinking, "I'm not good enough," recognize this as an energy that can be transmuted. Visualize the Violet Flame surrounding this thought, dissolving its hold on your consciousness. As the flame works, replace the negative thought with an empowering one, such as, "I AM a divine being, worthy of love and success."

Repeat this process with any other thoughts or emotions that arise, allowing the Violet Flame to work on every level of your being.

As you continue to work with the Violet Flame, you will likely notice a shift in your energy and overall sense of well-being. Negative patterns, whether they are physical, emotional, mental, or karmic, will begin to dissolve, creating space for new, higher-vibrational energies to take their place. This process of transmutation is not a one-time event but an ongoing practice that deepens over time. The more consistently you work with the Violet Flame, the more you will align with its transformative power, leading to greater spiritual clarity, emotional peace, and physical vitality.

Emotional traumas often leave lasting imprints on our energy field. These traumas may be the result of painful experiences in relationships, family dynamics, or even childhood wounds. When unresolved, they create energetic blockages that can influence our present emotions, behaviors, and decisions. The Violet Flame offers a pathway for releasing these emotional wounds, freeing us from the past and allowing us to step into a state of emotional freedom and peace.

To begin healing emotional traumas with the Violet Flame, it's important to bring awareness to the emotions that have been buried or suppressed. This can be challenging, as many of us have learned to avoid uncomfortable emotions like grief, anger, or shame. However, the healing process requires that we face these emotions with compassion and allow them to surface for transformation. Take a moment to sit quietly and reflect on any emotional pain or unresolved issues you may be carrying. You may want to focus on a specific relationship, event, or pattern in your life where emotional healing is needed.

Once you have identified the emotional trauma you wish to heal, visualize the Violet Flame surrounding your heart center, where emotional energy is stored. Imagine the flame gently expanding through your chest, enveloping any emotional pain with its soft, violet light. As the flame works, allow yourself to fully feel the emotions that arise. Whether it's sadness, anger, or fear, let the emotions move through you without judgment. The Violet Flame will transmute these heavy energies into light, allowing them to be released from your heart and energy field.

As you visualize the Violet Flame working on your emotions, repeat the decree: "I AM the Violet Flame, transmuting all emotional pain and freeing my heart." With each repetition, feel the intensity of the emotions beginning to dissipate, replaced by a sense of peace and calm. This process may take time, especially if the emotional trauma is deep-rooted. Be patient with yourself and trust that the Violet Flame is working at the most appropriate pace for your healing.

Emotional healing with the Violet Flame is a gradual process that may need to be repeated several times to fully release the layers of pain. You may find it helpful to keep a journal of your emotions and the healing work you are doing, noting any changes in how you feel or how your relationships and behaviors shift over time. As the emotional blockages clear, you will likely notice a greater sense of emotional balance and resilience in your daily life.

In addition to healing emotional wounds, the Violet Flame can also be used to dissolve negative behavioral patterns that stem from these wounds. Behavioral patterns are the habitual ways we react to situations, often unconsciously, based on past experiences. For example, someone who has experienced betrayal may develop a pattern of mistrust, even in situations where there is no reason to doubt others. These patterns can limit our growth, prevent us from forming healthy relationships, and keep us trapped in cycles of negativity.

To begin dissolving negative behavioral patterns with the Violet Flame, start by identifying a pattern you wish to transform. This could be a pattern of self-sabotage, fear-based thinking, or destructive habits. Reflect on how this pattern has shown up in your life and the emotions that are tied to it. Once you have clarity on the pattern, call upon the Violet Flame to assist in its transmutation.

Visualize the Violet Flame surrounding your entire body, with a particular focus on your mind and energy field, where these patterns are stored. See the flame moving through your thoughts, beliefs, and behaviors, dissolving the energetic imprints of the pattern at its root. As the flame works, you may experience memories or emotions associated with the pattern rising to the surface. Acknowledge these feelings without judgment, and allow the Violet Flame to transform them into light.

Repeat the decree: "I AM the Violet Flame, transmuting all negative patterns and restoring my divine freedom." Feel the energy of the Violet Flame shifting the old behavioral patterns, making space for new, positive ways of being. As the pattern dissolves, you can reinforce the healing by replacing the negative behavior with a positive affirmation or intention. For example, if you are working to dissolve a pattern of self-doubt, you might replace it with the affirmation: "I trust in my abilities and the divine plan for my life."

This process of transmuting behavioral patterns with the Violet Flame is ongoing, as many patterns have developed over years and may not be resolved in one session. The key is to be consistent in your practice, using the Violet Flame regularly to continue clearing the layers of conditioning that have been built up over time. With each session, you will find that the intensity of the pattern diminishes, and you become more aligned with your true, divine nature.

In addition to personal emotional healing, the Violet Flame can also be used to assist others in their healing journey. If you are working with someone who is struggling with emotional trauma or negative patterns, you can call upon the Violet Flame to transmute the energies affecting them. Begin by visualizing the person surrounded by a column of violet light, with the intention of transmuting their emotional pain or behavioral blockages. As you hold this visualization, repeat the decree: "I AM the Violet Flame, transmuting all negative energies for [person's name] and restoring them to divine harmony."

It's important to remember that when working with others, you are not imposing your will upon them but simply offering the healing energy of the Violet Flame for their highest good. Trust that the Violet Flame will work in the way that is most appropriate for their healing, even if the results are not immediately visible. Always approach this work with an attitude of love, compassion, and non-attachment to the outcome.

Another powerful way to apply the Violet Flame for deep emotional and karmic healing is through forgiveness. Forgiveness is a transformative process that allows us to release the emotional burdens of resentment, anger, and guilt. These emotions, when left unaddressed, create energetic blockages that prevent us from moving forward in life. The Violet Flame can be used to facilitate the process of forgiveness, helping us to release the emotional ties that keep us connected to past hurts and open ourselves to new possibilities.

To use the Violet Flame for forgiveness, focus on a person or situation where you feel unresolved anger, resentment, or hurt. Visualize the Violet Flame surrounding both you and the other person, creating a space of divine light between you. As the flame works, imagine it dissolving the negative emotional cords that bind you to this situation, freeing both you and the other person from the weight of the past.

Repeat the decree: "I AM the Violet Flame of forgiveness, releasing all anger, resentment, and pain." As you say this, feel the burden of these emotions being lifted from your heart, replaced by a sense of peace and compassion. This process may take time, especially if the hurt runs deep, but with each repetition, the energy of the Violet Flame works to heal and release the emotional ties.

Forgiveness is not about condoning the actions of others or excusing harmful behavior, but about freeing yourself from the emotional weight of the experience. By using the Violet Flame, you create space for healing and new beginnings, both for yourself and for those involved. As the energy of forgiveness flows through you, you will likely find that you are able to approach life with a greater sense of openness, love, and acceptance.

The Violet Flame's ability to transmute emotional traumas, dissolve negative behavioral patterns, and facilitate forgiveness makes it an invaluable tool for personal transformation. By consistently working with this sacred energy, you can release the emotional burdens that have been weighing you down, heal deep-seated wounds, and open yourself to a more empowered, joyful way of being. As you integrate the Violet Flame into your daily life, you will find that emotional healing becomes a natural and ongoing process, leading to greater inner peace and spiritual growth.

Chapter 6
Healing Emotional and Karmic Wounds

Emotional and karmic wounds are among the most profound and challenging obstacles on the path to spiritual healing. These wounds often run deep, carrying the weight of both this lifetime's experiences and those accumulated from past incarnations. According to Saint Germain's teachings, healing these wounds is essential for achieving emotional freedom, spiritual evolution, and alignment with the divine purpose. The Violet Flame, as a tool for transmutation, plays a crucial role in releasing the emotional and karmic burdens that prevent us from fully stepping into our highest potential.

Emotional wounds typically stem from painful or traumatic experiences, especially those related to relationships, loss, betrayal, or unresolved grief. These experiences leave energetic imprints in the body and mind, creating blockages that affect our emotional well-being and influence how we navigate future relationships and situations. When emotional wounds are not addressed, they manifest as recurring patterns of fear, anger, or avoidance, ultimately limiting our ability to experience love, trust, and peace.

Karmic wounds, on the other hand, are deeper, often extending beyond our current lifetime. Karma is the spiritual law of cause and effect, where our past actions, thoughts, and intentions create consequences that we carry with us through lifetimes. Karmic wounds may manifest as recurring challenges, difficult relationships, or unexplained emotional reactions that seem disproportionate to the current situation. These karmic imprints are like energetic knots, tied to unresolved issues from the past, and can significantly influence the course of our lives until they are healed and released.

To begin healing emotional and karmic wounds, the first step is to acknowledge and become aware of the patterns or issues that keep resurfacing. Awareness is key because these wounds often operate from the subconscious, affecting our behavior and emotional responses without our full understanding. Take a moment to reflect on areas of your life where you experience repeated emotional pain, conflict, or limitations. These patterns might appear in your relationships, career, or personal growth. Recognizing them is the first step toward healing.

Once you've identified the emotional or karmic wounds you wish to heal, the next step is to invoke the transformative power of the Violet Flame. Begin by creating a quiet, sacred space for yourself where you can focus on this deep healing work. Sit comfortably, close your eyes, and take several deep breaths, allowing your body and mind to relax. Visualize a radiant violet light descending from above, surrounding your entire body. This violet light represents the Violet Flame, which will transmute the energetic blockages associated with your emotional and karmic wounds.

As the Violet Flame surrounds you, bring your awareness to the specific emotional or karmic wound you wish to address. It could be a memory of a past hurt, a recurring relationship dynamic, or an ongoing emotional pattern, such as fear of abandonment or low self-worth. Visualize the Violet Flame penetrating this wound, dissolving the heavy, stagnant energy associated with it. As the flame works, imagine the emotional pain or karmic burden being lifted from your heart and energy field.

Repeat the decree: "I AM the Violet Flame, transmuting all emotional and karmic wounds and restoring my divine freedom." As you repeat this decree, feel the energy of the Violet Flame working deeply within you, releasing the pain and clearing the karmic imprints from your soul's energy field. This process may stir up intense emotions or memories, which is a natural part of the healing. Allow these feelings to arise without judgment, trusting that the Violet Flame is dissolving them at their root.

For emotional wounds, it is essential to acknowledge the feelings that arise as part of the healing process. Whether it's grief, anger, sadness, or even guilt, these emotions need to be felt and processed to be fully released. You can use the Violet Flame as a gentle companion during this emotional release, visualizing it surrounding your heart and gently dissolving the pain. You may find it helpful to journal about the emotions that come up during this process, as writing can provide clarity and further facilitate the release of these energies.

When working with karmic wounds, the process may feel more subtle but equally powerful. Karmic wounds are often tied to past-life experiences or unresolved spiritual lessons that we carry forward into this lifetime. These wounds can manifest as recurring challenges, such as chronic health issues, difficult relationships, or repeated failures. To heal these karmic patterns, use the Violet Flame to clear the energetic ties to past lifetimes and dissolve the karmic residue that is influencing your present life.

A specific practice for addressing karmic wounds involves working with forgiveness. Forgiveness is a key element in the transmutation of karmic energies, as it releases the attachments that keep us bound to past actions and experiences. Begin by focusing on the individual or situation where karmic pain exists. This may be a person from your current life, or you may have an intuitive sense that it relates to a past-life connection. Visualize the Violet Flame surrounding both you and the other person, dissolving the energetic cords of resentment, guilt, or unresolved conflict.

Repeat the decree: "I AM the Violet Flame of forgiveness, releasing all karmic debts and restoring divine harmony." With each repetition, feel the energy of the Violet Flame clearing the karmic ties between you and the other person or situation. This process may take time, especially if the karmic wound is deeply rooted, but with consistent practice, the Violet Flame will dissolve the energetic blockages, allowing you to release the past and move forward.

In addition to forgiveness, self-compassion is an essential aspect of healing karmic wounds. Many of us carry karmic imprints of guilt or unworthiness from past lifetimes, where we may have made choices that we now regret on a soul level. The Violet Flame can assist in healing these feelings of guilt or shame by transmuting the energy into self-acceptance and love. Visualize the Violet Flame enveloping your entire body, particularly around your heart and solar plexus, which are the centers for emotional healing and personal power.

As the flame works, repeat the decree: "I AM the Violet Flame, releasing all guilt and embracing my divine worth." Feel the heavy emotions lifting from your energy field, replaced by a sense of peace and self-compassion. This process allows you to free yourself from the karmic burdens of the past, opening the way for greater spiritual growth and personal freedom.

It's important to recognize that healing emotional and karmic wounds is not an instant process. These wounds are often layered and require time, patience, and repeated attention to fully release. The Violet Flame is a powerful ally in this work, but it's essential to approach the process with compassion for yourself and a willingness to engage in ongoing healing. Each time you work with the Violet Flame, you clear another layer of pain, allowing for deeper levels of transformation and renewal.

Another practice that supports the healing of emotional and karmic wounds is the use of decrees alongside meditation. Decrees, which are powerful spoken affirmations, help to direct the energy of the Violet Flame toward specific areas of healing. As you sit in meditation, focus on the wound or pattern you are healing and repeat a decree such as: "I AM the Violet Flame, transmuting all emotional wounds and freeing myself from the past." The repetition of this decree helps to reinforce your intention and align your energy with the Violet Flame's transformative power.

The healing of emotional and karmic wounds through the Violet Flame is one of the most profound aspects of Saint Germain's teachings. As you continue to engage in this work, you will likely notice significant shifts in your emotional well-being, relationships, and spiritual path. Old patterns that once held you back will dissolve, making way for new opportunities, deeper relationships, and a greater sense of purpose and freedom in your life.

Through the regular practice of invoking the Violet Flame, you not only heal the wounds of the past but also align more fully with your divine potential. This process of emotional and karmic transmutation leads to a sense of wholeness, where you are no longer defined by the pain of the past but are empowered to create a future rooted in love, peace, and spiritual fulfillment.

The healing of emotional and karmic wounds, is an ongoing process that unfolds over time. The Violet Flame plays a key role in dissolving the energetic imprints and emotional blockages that have built up over lifetimes. In this part, we will focus on more advanced and practical techniques for emotional healing and karmic release, offering ways to use the Violet Flame to heal deeply ingrained emotional patterns, resolve karmic debts, and release attachments to past-life experiences that still influence the present.

One of the most powerful applications of the Violet Flame is its ability to dissolve emotional contracts—unspoken agreements formed between individuals based on emotional or karmic ties. These contracts often arise in relationships where there is a history of unresolved emotions, such as dependency, guilt, or obligation. Over time, these emotional contracts can become energetically binding, making it difficult to move forward or break free from repetitive relational patterns. The Violet Flame offers a means of dissolving these contracts, freeing both parties from the energetic entanglement and allowing for greater clarity and freedom in the relationship.

To begin dissolving emotional contracts with the Violet Flame, sit in a quiet space where you can focus without interruption. Take a few deep breaths, bringing your awareness to the relationship or emotional tie you wish to release. Visualize the person with whom you have this emotional contract standing in front of you. As you do this, remain mindful of any emotions that arise—whether they are feelings of anger, guilt, love, or resentment. These emotions are part of the energetic contract that needs to be released.

Call upon the Violet Flame to assist in this process by visualizing a brilliant violet light surrounding both you and the other person. See the Violet Flame enveloping the energetic cords that connect you, dissolving the emotional and karmic ties that have bound you together. As the flame works, imagine the energy of the relationship being purified, releasing both of you from the weight of the past. You may feel a sense of lightness or emotional relief as the contract dissolves.

Repeat the decree: "I AM the Violet Flame, dissolving all emotional contracts and restoring divine freedom." With each repetition, feel the Violet Flame transmuting the energy of the relationship, clearing away any unresolved emotions or karmic imprints. As the contract dissolves, you may wish to bless the other person and yourself with love and forgiveness, acknowledging the lessons learned from the relationship while releasing any lingering emotional attachments.

This practice can be repeated for any relationships or emotional ties that feel energetically binding. It is especially useful for relationships where there has been long-standing conflict, dependency, or unresolved emotional pain. The Violet Flame not only dissolves the energetic contract but also heals the emotional wounds that created the contract in the first place, allowing both individuals to move forward in peace and freedom.

In addition to dissolving emotional contracts, the Violet Flame can also be used to release karmic ties that extend beyond this lifetime. Karmic ties are energetic connections formed through past-life interactions, where unresolved issues or imbalances remain. These ties can manifest in the present as recurring relationship dynamics, feelings of inexplicable guilt or obligation, or repetitive life challenges that seem beyond our control. By working with the Violet Flame, we can release these karmic ties and restore balance to our soul's journey.

To release karmic ties with the Violet Flame, begin by focusing on a specific area of your life where you feel stuck or where repetitive patterns seem to play out. This could be a relationship, a health issue, or a recurring emotional state, such as fear or insecurity. As you reflect on this pattern, call upon the Violet Flame to transmute the karmic energy underlying the situation. Visualize a violet light surrounding the entire situation, dissolving the karmic ties that have kept you bound to this pattern.

Repeat the decree: "I AM the Violet Flame, transmuting all karmic ties and restoring divine harmony." As you repeat this decree, imagine the karmic energy being lifted from your soul, freeing you from the cycle of repetition and allowing for new possibilities to emerge. You may experience a sense of emotional release or clarity as the karmic energy dissolves. Trust that the Violet Flame is working not only on the surface level but at the soul level, clearing the karmic imprints that have influenced your current experience.

For more advanced karmic healing, you can work with past-life regression techniques alongside the Violet Flame. Past-life regression involves accessing memories or energies from previous lifetimes that are still affecting your present reality. While this process can be done with the help of a trained therapist, you can also engage in a simpler form of past-life exploration through meditation and visualization.

Begin by entering a deep meditative state, using breathwork to relax and center yourself. Once you are in a calm and receptive state, ask your higher self or spiritual guides to reveal a past-life memory or karmic pattern that is ready to be healed. You may receive an image, feeling, or intuitive knowing about a particular lifetime or experience. Trust whatever comes through, even if it is vague at first.

As you connect with this past-life memory, visualize the Violet Flame surrounding both you and the past-life experience. Imagine the flame dissolving any karmic debts, unresolved emotions, or energetic ties that have carried over into this lifetime. Repeat the decree: "I AM the Violet Flame, transmuting all past-life karma and restoring divine balance." With each repetition, feel the karmic energy being lifted and cleared from your energy field, freeing you from the influence of this past experience.

You can conclude this practice by offering gratitude to your higher self and spiritual guides for their assistance in the healing process. As you come out of the meditation, take note of any insights or emotional shifts you experienced, and allow yourself time to integrate the healing.

Another significant application of the Violet Flame in karmic healing is the release of ancestral patterns. Ancestral patterns are energetic imprints passed down through generations, often manifesting as shared emotional or behavioral tendencies within families. These patterns can include fear, poverty consciousness, addiction, or unresolved trauma. While these patterns may not originate in your personal experience, they can influence your life and relationships in powerful ways.

To release ancestral patterns with the Violet Flame, begin by reflecting on any recurring issues or emotional dynamics within your family. You may notice patterns of behavior, belief systems, or emotional responses that seem to be passed down from generation to generation. Once you have identified the ancestral pattern you wish to heal, call upon the Violet Flame to transmute this energy on behalf of your lineage.

Visualize the Violet Flame surrounding not only yourself but also your entire ancestral line. See the flame moving through the generations, clearing the energetic imprints that have been passed down. You can visualize the faces of your ancestors if that helps to focus your intention, or simply imagine the energy of your lineage being purified by the flame. Repeat the decree: "I AM the Violet Flame, transmuting all ancestral patterns and restoring divine harmony to my lineage."

As the Violet Flame works, you may feel a sense of release, not only within yourself but also on behalf of your ancestors. This process can bring profound healing, as it not only frees you from the influence of ancestral patterns but also offers healing to your family lineage. Over time, you may notice shifts in your relationships with family members or in your personal emotional responses, as the weight of these inherited patterns is lifted.

The Violet Flame is an invaluable tool for both emotional and karmic healing, offering the power to dissolve the energetic imprints that limit our spiritual growth and personal freedom. Whether you are working to heal emotional wounds from this lifetime, release karmic debts from past lives, or transmute ancestral patterns, the Violet Flame provides a path toward greater emotional liberation and spiritual alignment.

As you continue to work with the Violet Flame, you will find that your emotional landscape begins to shift. Patterns that once seemed immovable will dissolve, making way for new experiences and opportunities. The release of karmic and emotional burdens allows for greater clarity, peace, and empowerment, ultimately aligning you more fully with your soul's purpose and the divine plan for your life.

By consistently invoking the Violet Flame and engaging in the practices outlined in this chapter, you will facilitate deep healing at every level of your being. The transformative power of the Violet Flame will help you transcend the limitations of the past, opening the door to a future filled with love, freedom, and spiritual growth.

Chapter 7
Self-Healing: Applying the Techniques to Yourself

Self-healing is one of the most empowering aspects of holistic healing, as it places the responsibility and power for transformation in your own hands. Saint Germain's teachings emphasize that self-healing not only brings physical health but also spiritual alignment, emotional balance, and mental clarity.

The first step in self-healing is learning to diagnose imbalances in your own energy field. This requires self-awareness and a willingness to tune into the subtle cues your body and mind provide. Imbalances in your energy field can manifest in various ways, including physical symptoms like fatigue or pain, emotional disturbances such as anxiety or sadness, or mental confusion and lack of focus. These imbalances often indicate blockages or stagnation in the energy centers, also known as chakras, which need to be addressed to restore harmony.

To begin diagnosing your energy field, take some time each day to sit quietly and perform a self-scan. Close your eyes and breathe deeply, allowing yourself to relax fully. Start at the top of your head and slowly move your awareness down through your body, paying attention to any areas where you feel tension, discomfort, or a sense of heaviness. These sensations can indicate where energy is not flowing freely and where healing is needed. As you perform this scan, be mindful of any emotions or thoughts that arise—often, emotional or mental patterns are closely linked to physical symptoms.

Once you have identified areas of imbalance, you can begin working with the Sacred Flames, particularly the Violet Flame, to transmute any blocked or negative energy. The Violet Flame is a powerful tool for self-healing because of its ability to dissolve lower vibrations and restore balance to the energy field. Visualize the Violet Flame surrounding your entire body, enveloping you in a radiant violet light. As you breathe, imagine this light entering the areas where you identified blockages or imbalances, gently dissolving any dense or stagnant energy.

As the Violet Flame works, repeat the decree: "I AM the Violet Flame, transmuting all that no longer serves me and restoring perfect health and balance." With each repetition, feel the energy in your body becoming lighter and more fluid, as the blockages are cleared and replaced with pure, high-frequency light. You may notice sensations of warmth, tingling, or even emotional release as the energy begins to shift. These are all signs that the Violet Flame is working on a deep level, restoring harmony to your energy field.

In addition to using the Violet Flame, it is important to incorporate the other Sacred Flames in your self-healing practice. The Blue Flame, representing divine will and protection, can be used to fortify your energy field and protect it from external influences. After using the Violet Flame to clear blockages, visualize the Blue Flame surrounding your body like a shield, creating a protective barrier that keeps your energy strong and resilient. Repeat the decree: "I AM the Blue Flame, protecting and strengthening my energy field." This practice not only protects you from negative energies but also reinforces your inner strength, making it easier to maintain balance.

The Pink Flame of love and compassion is particularly useful for emotional healing. If you are experiencing emotional pain or unresolved grief, visualize the Pink Flame surrounding your heart center. As the pink light fills your chest, feel it dissolving any emotional wounds, resentment, or fear. Repeat the decree: "I AM the Pink Flame of divine love, healing my heart and restoring emotional peace." As the Pink Flame works, you may experience a deep sense of comfort and relief, as the emotional weight is lifted and replaced with unconditional love and compassion.

The Green Flame, associated with physical healing and balance, is another essential tool for self-healing. If you are dealing with a specific physical ailment or health issue, visualize the Green Flame surrounding the affected area of your body. Imagine the green light penetrating deep into your cells, tissues, and organs, restoring health and vitality. Repeat the decree: "I AM the healing light of the Green Flame, restoring perfect health to my body." As the Green Flame works, you may feel a sense of renewal and strength in the physical body, as the energy of healing flows through you.

Incorporating these Sacred Flames into a daily self-healing practice can create profound shifts in your overall well-being. It is important to approach this practice with consistency and patience, as healing is often a gradual process that unfolds over time. By regularly scanning your energy field, working with the Sacred Flames, and addressing imbalances as they arise, you will create a foundation for long-term health and spiritual growth.

Self-healing also involves cultivating a deeper connection with your inner self. Saint Germain's teachings emphasize that the true source of healing lies within, and by aligning with your higher self, you can access the divine wisdom and energy needed for transformation. Meditation is a powerful tool for strengthening this connection. Through meditation, you quiet the mind and open yourself to receive guidance from your higher self and spiritual guides. This guidance often comes in the form of intuitive insights, dreams, or subtle feelings that direct you toward the areas of your life that need healing.

A simple meditation for self-healing involves connecting with your heart center, which is the seat of your higher self. Sit in a quiet place and close your eyes, bringing your awareness to your heart. As you breathe deeply, imagine a soft, glowing light in the center of your chest. This light represents the energy of your higher self, which is always present and available to guide and heal you. As you focus on this light, ask your higher self to reveal any areas of your life—whether physical, emotional, or spiritual—that need healing.

You may receive an image, feeling, or thought that indicates where your focus should be. Trust whatever comes through, knowing that your higher self is guiding you toward the next step in your healing journey. As you continue to breathe, visualize the Sacred Flames working in harmony to address the area that needs healing. Allow the Violet Flame to clear away any blockages, the Blue Flame to protect and fortify your energy, the Pink Flame to heal emotional wounds, and the Green Flame to restore physical balance.

As you come out of the meditation, take a few moments to reflect on any insights or sensations you experienced. You may want to keep a journal to record your experiences, as this can provide valuable guidance for your ongoing self-healing practice. Over time, you will notice that your connection to your higher self becomes stronger, and your ability to heal yourself deepens.

Another important aspect of self-healing is practicing self-care and nurturing your physical body. While the Sacred Flames work on the energetic and spiritual levels, it is essential to support the healing process by caring for your physical health. This includes eating nourishing foods, staying hydrated, getting enough rest, and engaging in physical activity that supports your body's natural healing processes. The physical body is the vessel for your spiritual energy, and by treating it with care and respect, you create the optimal conditions for healing and growth.

Incorporating grounding practices into your self-healing routine is also essential. Grounding helps to stabilize your energy and anchor the healing you are doing on a spiritual level into your physical body and daily life. Simple grounding techniques include walking barefoot on the earth, spending time in nature, or using visualization to imagine roots extending from your feet into the ground. These practices help to integrate the energy of the Sacred Flames into your physical experience, ensuring that the healing is not only energetic but also manifests in tangible ways.

Through consistent self-healing practices, you will experience a deeper sense of empowerment and alignment with your true self. The more you work with the Sacred Flames and develop your ability to diagnose and heal your own energy, the more you will open yourself to the flow of divine energy and wisdom. As you heal yourself, you also raise your vibrational frequency, making it easier to maintain balance and attract positive experiences into your life.

The journey of self-healing is an ongoing process of self-discovery and spiritual growth. By applying the techniques taught by Saint Germain, including the use of the Sacred Flames, meditation, and grounding, you can transform your energy, heal your body and mind, and align with your highest potential.

These exercises are designed to help you become more attuned to your body and energy field, empowering you to apply healing methods directly and consistently. By establishing a regular self-healing practice, you can maintain energetic balance, increase your spiritual awareness, and deepen your relationship with your inner self and the divine energy of Saint Germain.

One of the most effective ways to structure a self-healing session is through a ritual that involves intentional cleansing, alignment, and transmutation of energies. This process combines the power of the Sacred Flames with meditation and energy work, offering a holistic approach that addresses physical, emotional, mental, and spiritual layers. The following is a step-by-step guide for conducting a self-healing session using these techniques:

Preparation and Intention Setting: Begin your session by creating a sacred space. This can be a quiet, comfortable place in your home where you will not be disturbed. You may want to light a candle, burn incense, or play soft music to enhance the atmosphere. Once you have prepared the space, sit comfortably and close your eyes. Take several deep breaths, allowing yourself to relax and let go of any tension. Set a clear intention for your healing session. For example, you might say, "I intend to heal and release any imbalances in my energy field and restore harmony to my body, mind, and spirit."

Auric Cleansing with the Violet Flame: Once you have set your intention, visualize the Violet Flame surrounding your entire body and aura. See this flame as a vibrant violet light that gently moves through your energy field, dissolving any negative or stagnant energy. As the flame works, focus on any areas of your body or aura that feel heavy or blocked, allowing the Violet Flame to clear these areas. You may repeat the decree: "I AM the Violet Flame, transmuting all negative energies and restoring purity and balance to my being." As you continue to visualize the flame, feel your energy field becoming lighter and more vibrant.

Chakra Alignment: After cleansing your aura, the next step is to align and balance your chakras. Chakras are the energy centers of your body, and when they are aligned, energy flows freely, promoting health and well-being. Begin at the root chakra, located at the base of the spine. Visualize a deep red light spinning and growing brighter as the chakra becomes activated and balanced. Move upward to the sacral chakra (orange), solar plexus (yellow), heart (green), throat (blue), third eye (indigo), and crown (violet or white). As you visualize each chakra, see it spinning smoothly and radiating vibrant light. You may use the decree: "I AM aligned with the divine energy of the Sacred Flames, balancing and harmonizing all of my chakras."

Energy Transmutation with the Sacred Flames: Once your chakras are aligned, begin the process of transmuting any lingering negative energies, emotions, or patterns that are affecting your well-being. Focus on a specific issue or pattern that you wish to heal—this could be an emotional wound, a limiting belief, or a physical condition. Call upon the Violet Flame to transmute this energy at its root. Visualize the Violet Flame surrounding the issue, dissolving the negative energy and transforming it into light. You may repeat the decree: "I AM the Violet Flame, transmuting all that no longer serves me and transforming it into divine light and freedom." Allow yourself to feel the energy shifting as the flame works, releasing old patterns and creating space for new, higher vibrations.

Grounding and Integration: After the transmutation process, it is important to ground yourself and integrate the healing energy into your physical body and daily life. Grounding helps to anchor the spiritual energy you have worked with, ensuring that it manifests in a tangible way. To ground, visualize roots extending from your feet deep into the earth. As you breathe, imagine drawing up the Earth's stabilizing energy through these roots, filling your body with a sense of strength and stability. You may also repeat the decree: "I AM grounded and aligned with the Earth, fully integrated with divine energy." Spend a few moments in this grounded state, allowing the healing to settle into your entire being.

Closing the Session with Gratitude: To conclude your self-healing session, take a moment to express gratitude for the healing you have received. You can do this silently in your heart or aloud. A simple expression of thanks to the Violet Flame, the Sacred Flames, Saint Germain, and your higher self for their assistance and guidance will help to close the session on a positive note. As you end the session, you may feel lighter, more at peace, and aligned with your higher self. Be sure to drink water after the session to help with the energetic clearing and integration.

Regularly practicing these self-healing sessions will not only clear away negative energies but also strengthen your connection to your inner self and the divine energy available to you. Over time, you will notice that your energy becomes more balanced, and your physical, emotional, and spiritual health improves.

In addition to structured healing sessions, there are practical exercises that can be incorporated into daily life to maintain energetic balance and promote ongoing healing. These exercises are simple but effective, allowing you to consistently work with the Sacred Flames and the teachings of Saint Germain throughout your day.

Daily Aura Cleansing with the Violet Flame: One of the most important practices for maintaining energetic hygiene is the daily cleansing of your aura with the Violet Flame. This can be done quickly each morning or evening to clear away any negative or stagnant energy that may have accumulated throughout the day. Simply visualize the Violet Flame surrounding your entire body and aura, moving through each layer of your energy field and dissolving any impurities. You may use the decree: "I AM the Violet Flame, cleansing and purifying my energy field, restoring it to divine harmony." This practice helps to keep your energy field clear and free-flowing, preventing imbalances from taking root.

Heart-Centered Breathing for Emotional Balance: Emotional well-being is a key aspect of self-healing, and one of the simplest ways to maintain emotional balance is through heart-centered breathing. Whenever you feel emotionally overwhelmed or disconnected, place your hands over your heart and take several deep breaths, focusing on the energy of love and compassion. Visualize the Pink Flame of love surrounding your heart, dissolving any emotional pain or tension. Repeat the decree: "I AM filled with the love and compassion of the Pink Flame, healing all wounds and restoring peace to my heart." This exercise can be done anytime you need to center yourself emotionally, helping to bring a sense of calm and balance.

Chakra Tuning with Sound and Decrees: Another way to maintain energetic alignment is through sound healing combined with decrees. Each chakra resonates with a specific sound frequency, and by working with sound, you can activate and balance your energy centers. For example, chanting the sound "LAM" for the root chakra or "OM" for the third eye chakra can help bring these energy centers into alignment. As you chant, visualize the corresponding chakra spinning brightly and use a decree to reinforce the healing: "I AM aligned with divine energy, and my chakras are in perfect harmony." This practice is particularly useful for maintaining balance between healing sessions.

Grounding Through Nature: Spending time in nature is one of the most powerful ways to ground and restore your energy. Whenever you feel disconnected or energetically scattered, take a walk in nature, barefoot if possible, to reconnect with the Earth's natural rhythms. As you walk, visualize the energy of the Earth flowing up through your feet and into your body, stabilizing your energy and grounding your spiritual experiences into physical reality. You may use the decree: "I AM grounded in the Earth's energy, fully present and aligned with my divine path."

Mindful Awareness and Presence: Lastly, practicing mindful awareness throughout the day is essential for maintaining energetic balance. By staying present in each moment, you become more aware of your thoughts, emotions, and energy, making it easier to recognize when something is out of balance. Whenever you notice yourself becoming distracted or overwhelmed, pause, take a deep breath, and bring your awareness back to the present moment. This simple practice helps to prevent energy drain and keeps you aligned with your higher self.

By integrating these exercises and practices into your daily life, you will develop a greater sense of control over your energy, health, and spiritual well-being. Self-healing, as taught by Saint Germain, is a lifelong practice that empowers you to take charge of your personal transformation and align with your highest potential. As you continue to work with the Sacred Flames and refine your self-healing techniques, you will experience deeper levels of healing, clarity, and spiritual awakening, opening the door to a life filled with balance, peace, and divine purpose.

Chapter 8
Distance Healing: Theory and Fundamentals

The concept of distance healing is rooted in the understanding that energy is not bound by physical space or time. According to Saint Germain's teachings, the ability to send healing energy across distances is a natural extension of our spiritual connection to the divine and the universal flow of energy.

At its core, distance healing relies on the principle that we are all connected through a unified field of energy. This field, sometimes referred to as the "quantum field" or "universal consciousness," allows energy to flow freely between all living beings, regardless of geographical distance. Through intention, focus, and spiritual alignment, a healer can direct energy to a recipient anywhere in the world. Saint Germain teaches that the Sacred Flames, particularly the Violet Flame, are powerful tools for conducting distance healing, as they work across dimensions to transmute negative energies and restore balance in the energy field.

The first step in understanding distance healing is to recognize that energy exists beyond the physical body. Each person has an energy field, or aura, that extends beyond their physical form, and this energy field is constantly interacting with the surrounding environment and with other people's energy fields. When you perform distance healing, you are tuning into the recipient's energy field and directing healing energy to it. This process is not limited by space or time because energy itself is not limited by these factors. Distance healing, therefore, is a matter of intention and focused awareness, combined with the use of spiritual energy, such as the Violet Flame, to facilitate healing.

To begin practicing distance healing, it's important to cultivate a strong foundation in your own energy. Before you can send healing energy to someone else, you need to ensure that your energy is clear, balanced, and aligned. This is especially important in distance healing, as any energetic imbalances in the healer can affect the flow of energy to the recipient. Start by preparing yourself energetically through meditation and the use of the Sacred Flames. Take a few moments to ground yourself, cleanse your aura with the Violet Flame, and align your chakras to ensure that you are a clear and open channel for healing energy.

Once your energy is aligned, the next step is to focus on the recipient. To do this, begin by visualizing the person you wish to send healing energy to. You may choose to look at a picture of them, hold something that belongs to them, or simply think of them with clarity and love. The key here is to connect with the person's energy field through your intention. Remember that you are not imposing your will on the recipient but offering them the opportunity to receive healing energy. The recipient's higher self will always have the final say in whether or not to accept the energy, so it's important to approach the process with respect and non-attachment to the outcome.

Once you have focused on the recipient, it's time to set your intention for the healing. Intention is the driving force behind distance healing, as it directs the flow of energy toward a specific purpose. Your intention should be clear, positive, and aligned with the highest good of the recipient. For example, you might set an intention such as, "I intend to send healing energy to [recipient's name], supporting their physical, emotional, and spiritual well-being." You can also tailor your intention to address specific issues, such as physical pain, emotional trauma, or energetic blockages.

After setting your intention, call upon the Violet Flame or any of the other Sacred Flames to assist in the healing process. Visualize a column of Violet Flame descending from above and surrounding the recipient. See the flame enveloping their entire body and energy field, gently dissolving any negative energies, blockages, or imbalances. As you hold this visualization, repeat the decree: "I AM the Violet Flame, transmuting all negative energies and restoring balance and harmony to [recipient's name]." Feel the energy of the Violet Flame flowing from you to the recipient, filling their energy field with healing light.

It's important to remain focused and present during the distance healing process. You may notice sensations such as warmth, tingling, or a sense of connection with the recipient as the energy flows. Trust that the Violet Flame is working at the deepest levels of the recipient's energy field, even if you don't receive immediate feedback. The healing energy will go where it is most needed, and the recipient's higher self will guide the process to ensure that it is aligned with their highest good.

One of the key aspects of distance healing is the understanding that time is not linear in the spiritual realm. This means that you can send healing energy not only to someone in the present moment but also to someone in the past or the future. For example, you might send healing energy to a loved one who experienced a traumatic event in the past, or you might send energy ahead to support someone facing a difficult situation in the future. The Violet Flame, as a transmutational tool, works across time and space, allowing you to address and heal energies from any point in time.

To send healing energy to the past, focus on the specific event or time period where the healing is needed. Visualize the Violet Flame surrounding the past version of the recipient and the situation, dissolving any negative energies or trauma associated with it. Use a decree such as, "I AM the Violet Flame, healing and transmuting all energies from the past, restoring peace and harmony to [recipient's name]." This practice helps to release the energetic imprints of past events, freeing the recipient from the lingering effects of trauma or pain.

Similarly, you can send healing energy to the future by focusing on an upcoming event or challenge. Visualize the recipient being surrounded by the Violet Flame during the future event, and set the intention that they are protected, balanced, and supported during that time. Use a decree like, "I AM the Violet Flame, protecting and guiding [recipient's name] in the future, ensuring their highest good and divine alignment." This practice helps to create a protective and supportive energetic foundation for the recipient as they move through future challenges.

An important aspect of distance healing is the practice of energetic boundaries. As a healer, it's essential to protect your own energy field during the process, especially when working with others. Before beginning any distance healing session, invoke the Blue Flame of protection to surround your energy field. Visualize a brilliant blue light enveloping your body, creating a protective shield that keeps your energy clear and prevents you from absorbing any negative or heavy energies from the recipient. Repeat the decree: "I AM the Blue Flame, protecting and fortifying my energy field as I send healing energy to [recipient's name]." This ensures that you remain energetically balanced and protected throughout the healing process.

Another technique for distance healing involves the use of objects or symbols to help focus and direct energy. For example, you might place your hands over a photograph of the recipient or hold a crystal that represents the person's energy. Some practitioners use symbols, such as a drawing of the recipient's body or a specific part of their energy field that needs healing, as a way to focus their intention. By directing energy toward these physical objects or symbols, you create a tangible connection between yourself and the recipient, making it easier to send healing energy across distances.

While distance healing is highly effective, it's important to remember that it is not a substitute for professional medical or psychological treatment. Instead, distance healing works in conjunction with other forms of healing to support the recipient's overall well-being. As a practitioner of distance healing, your role is to offer energetic support and spiritual assistance, knowing that the ultimate healing process is guided by the recipient's higher self and the divine.

It's important to close a distance healing session with gratitude and detachment. After you have completed the healing process, take a few moments to express gratitude to the Sacred Flames, Saint Germain, and your higher self for their assistance. Then, release the outcome of the healing to the universe, trusting that the energy has been received and will continue to work in alignment with the recipient's highest good. This practice of detachment helps you remain balanced and prevents you from becoming overly invested in the results of the healing.

Through the practice of distance healing, you can extend the power of the Sacred Flames to help others, regardless of where they are. By combining intention, visualization, and spiritual energy, you become a channel for divine healing energy that transcends physical space and time. As you continue to refine your distance healing techniques, you will experience deeper levels of connection, spiritual growth, and a greater understanding of the interconnectedness of all beings.

One of the simplest and most effective methods for distance healing involves using focused visualization combined with the energy of the Violet Flame. Visualization is a key component of distance healing, as it helps you to direct and amplify the healing energy you are sending. Through visualization, you create a clear mental image of the recipient and their energy field, which allows you to channel healing energy more precisely.

To begin a distance healing session with visualization, prepare yourself by sitting in a quiet, comfortable space where you can focus without distractions. Take a few deep breaths and ground yourself, feeling connected to the Earth's stabilizing energy. Once you feel centered, visualize the person you are sending healing energy to. You can imagine them sitting or standing in front of you, or you can hold a photograph or personal object belonging to the recipient to help you connect with their energy.

With a clear image of the recipient in your mind, visualize a column of Violet Flame descending from above and surrounding their entire body and energy field. See the Violet Flame moving through their physical body, dissolving any blockages or negative energies. As the flame works, imagine it clearing their chakras, healing emotional wounds, and restoring balance to their entire being. You may repeat the decree: "I AM the Violet Flame, transmuting all negative energies and restoring divine harmony to [recipient's name]." Continue holding this visualization for several minutes, focusing on the sensation of the Violet Flame working to heal and uplift the recipient.

In addition to visualizing the recipient's energy field being bathed in the Violet Flame, you can also focus on specific areas of their body or energy field that need extra attention. For example, if the recipient is experiencing physical pain in a particular part of their body, direct the Violet Flame to that area. Visualize the flame penetrating deep into the tissues, dissolving any blockages and restoring health and vitality. If the recipient is dealing with emotional pain, visualize the Violet Flame working in their heart center, gently healing the emotional wounds and releasing any feelings of sadness, fear, or anger.

Another powerful method for distance healing is the use of prayer and decrees. Decrees are affirmations spoken with intention and authority, calling upon divine energy to assist in the healing process. When you use decrees in distance healing, you are directing the flow of spiritual energy with precision, helping to focus and amplify the healing. Begin by setting a clear intention for the healing session. For example, if the recipient is in need of emotional healing, your intention might be, "I intend to send healing energy to [recipient's name] to support their emotional healing and well-being."

Once you have set your intention, begin repeating a decree that aligns with your goal. A common decree for distance healing is: "I AM the Violet Flame, healing and transmuting all energies in [recipient's name] and restoring them to divine balance." Repeat this decree several times, either silently or aloud, while focusing on the recipient. With each repetition, feel the energy of the Violet Flame flowing from you to the recipient, supporting their healing process. The repetition of the decree strengthens the energy being sent and helps to create a more powerful connection between you and the recipient's energy field.

For more advanced distance healing techniques, you can incorporate the use of sacred geometry or symbols into your practice. Sacred geometry involves using specific shapes and patterns that carry high vibrational frequencies, which can enhance the flow of healing energy. One common symbol used in distance healing is the "Merkaba," a three-dimensional geometric shape that represents the balance of spirit and matter and is believed to facilitate energetic healing and spiritual transformation.

To use the Merkaba in distance healing, visualize the recipient inside the center of a spinning Merkaba. Imagine the two interlocking pyramids of the Merkaba rotating in opposite directions, creating a vortex of healing energy around the recipient. As the Merkaba spins, visualize the Violet Flame filling the space inside, purifying the recipient's energy field and accelerating their healing process. You can also place the Merkaba over specific areas of the recipient's body that need healing, using it to concentrate the flow of energy in that area.

Another symbol that can be used in distance healing is the infinity symbol (∞), which represents the continuous flow of energy and the eternal nature of life. You can visualize the infinity symbol flowing through the recipient's energy field, helping to balance and harmonize their energy. Imagine the infinity symbol moving through their chakras, aligning and stabilizing each one. As you work with this symbol, repeat the decree: "I AM aligned with the infinite flow of divine energy, restoring balance and healing to [recipient's name]." This practice helps to create a steady and harmonious flow of energy within the recipient, supporting their healing journey.

It's important to protect your own energy while performing distance healing. As you connect with the recipient's energy field, you may inadvertently absorb some of their negative energies if you are not properly protected. Before beginning a distance healing session, call upon the Blue Flame of protection. Visualize a bright blue light surrounding your body and energy field, creating a protective shield that keeps your energy clear and separate from the recipient's energy. You may use the decree: "I AM the Blue Flame of divine protection, safeguarding my energy field as I send healing energy to [recipient's name]." This protective shield ensures that you remain energetically balanced throughout the healing session.

In some cases, you may wish to work with crystals during a distance healing session to amplify the energy being sent. Crystals have their own unique vibrational frequencies and can act as conduits for healing energy. Amethyst, for example, is a crystal closely connected to the Violet Flame and can be used to enhance the transmutational energy of the flame. To use crystals in distance healing, hold a crystal in your hand while focusing on the recipient's energy field. You can also place crystals around a photograph of the recipient or create a crystal grid with specific healing intentions. As you send healing energy, visualize the crystal amplifying the flow of energy and directing it toward the recipient.

Another practical method for distance healing is the use of energy cords or energetic ties. These cords represent the energetic connection between you and the recipient, allowing you to send healing energy directly through the cord. Begin by visualizing an energetic cord connecting your heart center to the heart center of the recipient. This cord acts as a channel for healing energy, allowing you to send love, compassion, and healing to the recipient. As you focus on the cord, visualize the Violet Flame traveling through it, dissolving any blockages or negative energies along the way. You may repeat the decree: "I AM the Violet Flame, sending healing energy through this cord to [recipient's name], restoring balance and harmony to their heart."

It's important to maintain a sense of detachment and trust when performing distance healing. While it's natural to want to see immediate results, the healing process unfolds according to the recipient's highest good and divine timing. After completing a distance healing session, take a moment to release your attachment to the outcome. Trust that the energy has been received and that it will continue to work on the recipient's energy field in the days and weeks to come. You may express gratitude to the Sacred Flames, your spiritual guides, and the recipient's higher self for their participation in the healing process.

To close the distance healing session, take a few deep breaths and ground yourself. You can visualize roots extending from your feet into the Earth, drawing up stabilizing energy to help you feel centered and balanced. As you come out of the healing session, you may feel lighter, more peaceful, and more connected to the divine flow of energy. Be sure to drink water afterward to help with the energetic integration and cleansing process.

Distance healing is a powerful way to offer support and healing to others, regardless of where they are located. By applying these practical methods, you can enhance your ability to work with the Sacred Flames, deepen your connection to the recipient, and create meaningful transformation in their energy field. Whether you are working with visualization, decrees, sacred geometry, or crystals, the most important element of distance healing is your intention and the purity of the energy you are sending. As you continue to develop your distance healing skills, you will find that your ability to channel divine energy becomes stronger and more refined, allowing you to be of greater service to others on their healing journey.

Chapter 9
The Power of the Spoken Word and Decrees in Healing

The spoken word carries immense power, not only in our daily lives but also in spiritual healing practices. Saint Germain's teachings emphasize the use of decrees—spoken affirmations that channel divine energy and activate the healing power of the Sacred Flames. Decrees work by aligning the individual's thoughts, emotions, and energy with the higher vibrations of divine light. When spoken with intention and conviction, decrees become powerful tools for transmuting negative energies, amplifying healing, and manifesting positive outcomes.

The vibration of words, especially when infused with intention, affects our energy field and the energy fields of others. The words we speak have the power to shape our reality, and in the context of healing, they can direct energy toward areas that need balance and transformation. Decrees harness this power by invoking divine energies, such as the Violet Flame, to work on specific issues or situations. Through repetition and focused intention, decrees help to reprogram the subconscious mind, clear energetic blockages, and raise the vibration of the individual or the situation being addressed.

At the core of Saint Germain's teachings on decrees is the use of the phrase "I AM." This phrase is more than just a simple affirmation; it is a declaration of alignment with the divine presence within. In the context of decrees, "I AM" signifies the embodiment of divine energy and the individual's connection to the Source of all creation. By beginning a decree with "I AM," the practitioner affirms their unity with the divine and activates the healing power of the Sacred Flames within themselves.

One of the most well-known and powerful decrees in Saint Germain's teachings is: "I AM a being of Violet Fire, I AM the purity God desires." This decree invokes the transformative power of the Violet Flame, calling upon it to transmute all negative energies within the individual's energy field and restore divine purity. The repetition of this decree creates a vibrational resonance that aligns the practitioner's energy with the higher frequencies of the Violet Flame, allowing for deep healing and transformation.

To effectively use decrees in healing, it is important to understand the principles of intention, focus, and repetition. Intention is the driving force behind any decree, as it directs the flow of energy toward a specific goal. Before beginning a decree, take a moment to set a clear and positive intention for the healing. This intention might be to transmute negative energy, heal emotional wounds, restore balance to the chakras, or bring clarity to a challenging situation. Whatever the intention, it should always be aligned with the highest good of the individual or situation being addressed.

Once the intention is set, focus becomes the next key element. As you speak the decree, it is important to maintain full concentration on the energy you are invoking and the outcome you wish to manifest. Visualization can be a helpful tool in this process. For example, if you are using the Violet Flame for healing, visualize the violet light surrounding your body or the person you are sending healing to as you speak the decree. See the energy of the flame dissolving any negative energies and filling the space with light. This focus strengthens the connection between your spoken words and the divine energy, making the decree more effective.

Repetition is another important aspect of working with decrees. The vibrational power of the decree builds with each repetition, amplifying the energy being directed toward the intention. Decrees are often repeated three, seven, or nine times, as these numbers are considered spiritually significant and help to deepen the alignment with divine energy. As you repeat the decree, feel the energy expanding and becoming stronger with each recitation. The repetition creates a rhythm that aligns your mind, body, and spirit with the higher vibrations of the Sacred Flames.

Decrees can be used in a variety of healing contexts, from personal healing to sending healing energy to others, and even for planetary healing. One powerful decree for self-healing is: "I AM the healing light of the Green Flame, restoring perfect health to my body." This decree invokes the Green Flame, which is associated with physical healing and balance. As you repeat this decree, visualize the Green Flame surrounding your body, healing and restoring vitality to every cell, tissue, and organ. This practice can be particularly helpful for addressing specific physical ailments or for maintaining overall health and well-being.

For emotional healing, the following decree can be used: "I AM the Pink Flame of divine love, healing all wounds and restoring emotional peace." The Pink Flame is associated with love, compassion, and emotional healing. As you speak this decree, visualize the Pink Flame surrounding your heart center, gently dissolving any emotional pain or wounds. Feel the energy of the Pink Flame filling your heart with unconditional love and compassion, allowing you to release any feelings of hurt, anger, or fear. This decree is especially effective for healing relationships, grief, or any emotional trauma that has left an imprint on your heart.

In addition to personal healing, decrees can be used to send healing energy to others. For example, if someone you know is experiencing physical or emotional challenges, you can use a decree to direct the energy of the Sacred Flames to them. A simple but powerful decree for this purpose is: "I AM the Violet Flame, transmuting all negative energies in [recipient's name] and restoring divine balance and harmony." As you speak this decree, visualize the Violet Flame surrounding the person, clearing away any negative energies and restoring balance to their energy field. This practice can be done remotely, making it an effective tool for distance healing.

Decrees can also be used to address specific situations, challenges, or patterns in your life. For example, if you are dealing with a recurring negative pattern, such as self-doubt or fear, you can use a decree to transmute the energy of that pattern and replace it with a higher vibration. A decree for transmuting negative patterns might be: "I AM the Violet Flame, dissolving all patterns of fear and replacing them with divine confidence and peace." As you repeat this decree, visualize the Violet Flame dissolving the energetic imprints of fear or doubt and replacing them with the energy of confidence, peace, and trust in the divine plan.

Another practical application of decrees is in the protection and cleansing of physical spaces. Spaces, like people, accumulate energy over time, and if that energy is not regularly cleared, it can become stagnant or negative. To cleanse and protect a space, you can use a decree such as: "I AM the Violet Flame, purifying this space and filling it with divine light and peace." As you repeat this decree, visualize the Violet Flame sweeping through every corner of the space, dissolving any negative or stagnant energies and replacing them with pure, high-vibrational light. This practice helps to maintain a harmonious and uplifting environment, whether it's your home, workplace, or any space where healing is needed.

It's important to remember that decrees are most effective when spoken with conviction and belief. The energy behind the words is what gives them their power, so speak each decree with confidence, knowing that you are aligning yourself with divine energy. Decrees can be spoken aloud, silently, or even written down and repeated mentally throughout the day. The key is to maintain focus and intention, allowing the energy of the decree to work on a deep level, both within yourself and in the world around you.

As you continue to work with decrees, you will find that they become a natural and powerful part of your healing practice. Whether you are using decrees for personal healing, sending healing energy to others, or addressing specific challenges, the spoken word has the power to activate the divine energy of the Sacred Flames and bring about profound transformation. Over time, you will notice shifts in your energy, emotions, and circumstances as the decrees work to align you more fully with your highest good and the flow of divine light.

The beauty of decrees lies in their versatility. While there are many established decrees, such as those used to invoke the Violet Flame or specific Sacred Flames, you can also create personalized decrees that resonate with your unique intentions and needs. A personalized decree combines the basic structure of a traditional decree—starting with the powerful "I AM" phrase—with specific language that reflects your goals, whether it's healing, emotional balance, or spiritual growth. The process of creating your own decree allows you to focus deeply on the energy you wish to invoke, making the decree even more effective.

To create a personalized decree, begin by reflecting on the issue or intention you want to address. For example, if you are working on healing a specific physical ailment, your decree will focus on invoking the healing energy of the Sacred Flames to address that condition. If your goal is emotional healing or spiritual growth, your decree might call upon energies like love, peace, and divine wisdom to support you on your path.

Once you have a clear sense of your intention, start by crafting a simple but powerful affirmation that begins with "I AM." This phrase connects you directly to divine energy and affirms your alignment with the higher self. For example, if you are working on healing a chronic illness, you might say: "I AM the divine light of healing, restoring perfect health and vitality to my body." If you are focusing on emotional healing, a decree might be: "I AM the Pink Flame of divine love, healing all emotional wounds and filling my heart with peace."

After establishing the core of your decree, you can refine it further by adding details specific to the situation. If you are working on a physical ailment, specify the area of the body that needs healing. For example: "I AM the Green Flame of divine healing, restoring health and balance to my lungs, filling each breath with life-giving energy." If you are focusing on a mental or emotional challenge, tailor the decree to address the specific emotions or thoughts involved. For example: "I AM the Violet Flame, dissolving all patterns of fear and replacing them with divine trust and confidence."

The key to creating effective personalized decrees is to keep the language clear, direct, and positive. Avoid focusing on the negative aspects of the situation (such as "I AM not sick" or "I AM free from pain") and instead, focus on the positive outcome you wish to manifest ("I AM filled with health and vitality" or "I AM strong and peaceful"). This positive focus aligns your energy with the desired outcome and reinforces the vibrational power of the decree.

Once you have crafted your personalized decree, it's time to integrate it into your healing practice. One of the most effective ways to use decrees is to repeat them regularly, either in meditation or throughout the day. The repetition of the decree helps to reprogram your subconscious mind and align your energy with the vibration of the words. As you repeat the decree, focus on the intention behind it, visualizing the energy of the Sacred Flames working in harmony with your words.

For example, if your decree focuses on physical healing, visualize the healing energy flowing through your body as you repeat the decree. Imagine the Green Flame or Violet Flame surrounding the area that needs healing, dissolving any blockages and restoring health and balance. If your decree is focused on emotional healing, visualize the Pink Flame surrounding your heart, gently releasing any emotional pain or wounds as you speak the words. The more vividly you can visualize the energy working alongside the decree, the more effective the process will be.

Incorporating decrees into daily spiritual practice is another powerful way to maintain energetic alignment and promote continuous healing. Start your day by repeating a series of decrees that align with your intentions. For example, you might begin with a general decree for protection, such as: "I AM the Blue Flame of divine protection, shielding my energy and guiding me throughout the day." Follow this with a decree for personal healing, like: "I AM the Violet Flame, transmuting all negative energies and restoring balance to my mind, body, and spirit."

You can also use decrees throughout the day whenever you feel your energy becoming imbalanced or when you need extra support. For instance, if you find yourself feeling anxious or stressed, take a moment to recenter yourself and speak a decree for peace and calm: "I AM the light of divine peace, releasing all anxiety and filling my heart with tranquility." This simple practice helps to realign your energy in the moment, ensuring that you stay connected to the higher vibrations of the Sacred Flames.

Decrees can also be used to address specific challenges or situations in your life, such as work-related stress, relationship issues, or financial concerns. When using decrees for these purposes, it's important to keep the focus on healing and transformation rather than control. For example, if you are facing a difficult relationship dynamic, instead of focusing on changing the other person, use the decree to shift the energy within yourself and the situation. A decree for healing relationships might be: "I AM the Violet Flame, dissolving all conflict and restoring love and harmony in my relationships."

Similarly, if you are working on abundance or financial stability, craft a decree that focuses on aligning with the energy of prosperity. For example: "I AM aligned with the flow of divine abundance, receiving all that I need with grace and ease." As you repeat this decree, visualize the energy of abundance flowing into your life, dissolving any feelings of lack or limitation.

One of the most powerful uses of decrees is in the realm of collective or planetary healing. Saint Germain teaches that the Sacred Flames, particularly the Violet Flame, can be used to transmute negative energies on a global scale, contributing to the healing and upliftment of the entire planet. To participate in planetary healing, you can create decrees that focus on sending healing energy to the Earth and all beings.

For example, you might use the decree: "I AM the Violet Flame, transmuting all negative energies on Earth and restoring divine harmony to the planet." As you speak this decree, visualize the Violet Flame sweeping across the Earth, dissolving fear, anger, and conflict, and replacing them with peace, love, and unity. This practice not only helps to elevate the collective consciousness but also strengthens your own connection to the divine and your role as a lightworker.

When working with decrees for planetary healing, it's important to approach the process with a sense of humility and non-attachment. Remember that you are not imposing your will on the world but aligning with the divine plan for the Earth's healing. Trust that the energy of the Sacred Flames will go where it is needed most and that your contribution is part of a larger, collective effort to uplift the planet.

Finally, it's important to end each session of working with decrees with a moment of gratitude. Take a few moments to thank the Sacred Flames, Saint Germain, your higher self, and any spiritual guides who assisted in the process. This expression of gratitude not only helps to close the session on a positive note but also strengthens your connection to the divine energies you have been working with.

Over time, as you continue to work with decrees, you will notice shifts in your energy, your circumstances, and your overall well-being. Decrees are powerful tools for healing and transformation, not only because of the energy they invoke but also because they help you to take an active role in your own healing journey. By consistently using decrees to align your thoughts, emotions, and energy with the higher vibrations of the Sacred Flames, you create a foundation for lasting healing, spiritual growth, and positive change in all areas of your life.

In summary, decrees offer a simple yet profound way to access and channel the energy of the Sacred Flames for healing and transformation. Whether you are working on personal healing, supporting others, or contributing to planetary healing, decrees provide a direct and effective way to align with divine energy and manifest positive outcomes. By incorporating decrees into your daily spiritual practice and using them with intention, focus, and repetition, you can unlock their full potential and experience the transformative power of the spoken word in your life.

Chapter 10
The Violet Flame and Physical Body Transformation

The Violet Flame's power extends not only to the energetic and emotional bodies but also to the physical body. Saint Germain's teachings emphasize that by working with the Violet Flame, we can initiate profound transformations at the cellular level, revitalizing the body and promoting physical health

The physical body is deeply connected to the mind and spirit, and any imbalance in these areas can eventually manifest as physical illness or discomfort. The Violet Flame, known for its transformative and purifying properties, works by transmuting the lower energies and toxins that may accumulate in the body over time. These energies can come from external sources, such as environmental pollutants or unhealthy habits, or they may result from internal imbalances, such as negative thoughts or unresolved emotional issues. The Violet Flame clears these lower vibrations, allowing the body's natural state of health to emerge.

One of the fundamental ways the Violet Flame works on the physical body is through purification at the cellular level. Every cell in the body holds energy, and over time, cells can become burdened with toxins, stress, or stagnant energy. This buildup can affect the functioning of the body's systems, leading to fatigue, illness, or physical discomfort. By invoking the Violet Flame, you can direct this transmutational energy to cleanse and energize your cells, promoting renewal and healing.

To begin using the Violet Flame for physical body transformation, start by creating a quiet, peaceful environment where you can focus on your healing work. Sit or lie down comfortably and close your eyes, taking a few deep breaths to relax and center yourself. Visualize a column of Violet Flame descending from above, surrounding your entire body. As the flame envelops you, imagine it gently penetrating your skin and moving through your entire body, from your muscles and bones to your cells and organs.

As you hold this visualization, set the intention to purify your body at the cellular level. You might say, "I invoke the Violet Flame to purify and cleanse every cell in my body, transmuting all toxins and lower energies into light." As you repeat this intention, visualize the Violet Flame dissolving any stagnant energy or toxins in your body, releasing them into the light. You may feel warmth, tingling, or a sense of lightness as the energy begins to work. Trust that the Violet Flame is clearing away anything that no longer serves your physical health, allowing your cells to rejuvenate and function optimally.

In addition to general body purification, the Violet Flame can be directed to specific areas of the body that need healing or restoration. If you are experiencing pain, discomfort, or illness in a particular part of your body, focus the energy of the Violet Flame on that area. For example, if you are dealing with a digestive issue, visualize the Violet Flame surrounding your stomach and digestive system, clearing away any blockages or toxins. As the flame works, imagine your digestive system being filled with light and vitality, restoring balance and ease.

You can enhance this process by repeating a healing decree, such as: "I AM the Violet Flame, transmuting all discord and restoring perfect health to my [specific area]." As you repeat this decree, visualize the energy of the Violet Flame working more deeply in the affected area, dissolving any negative energy and replacing it with pure, healing light. Continue this process for several minutes, allowing the energy to flow freely through the area until you feel a sense of relief or balance.

The Violet Flame can also be used to revitalize the body's organs and systems, particularly those that may be overburdened by toxins or stress. The liver, kidneys, and lymphatic system are key organs involved in detoxifying the body, and they can benefit greatly from the cleansing power of the Violet Flame. To work with the Violet Flame in this way, visualize the flame surrounding these organs, gently purifying and renewing them. As the flame works, imagine any toxins or blockages being transmuted into light, and see the organs functioning with renewed vitality and strength.

Another important aspect of physical body transformation with the Violet Flame is working with the body's natural energy centers, or chakras. Each chakra is connected to specific organs and systems in the body, and when the chakras are blocked or imbalanced, this can lead to physical symptoms. By using the Violet Flame to clear and balance the chakras, you support the overall health and vitality of the body.

Begin by focusing on the root chakra, located at the base of the spine. Visualize the Violet Flame surrounding this chakra, dissolving any blockages or stagnant energy. As the flame works, feel the energy of the root chakra becoming more vibrant and balanced, supporting the health of your legs, bones, and lower body. Move upward through each chakra, using the Violet Flame to clear and energize the sacral chakra (connected to the reproductive and digestive systems), the solar plexus (related to digestion and metabolism), the heart chakra (linked to the circulatory and respiratory systems), the throat chakra (associated with the throat and lungs), the third eye (connected to the brain and nervous system), and finally the crown chakra (which governs the overall energy flow of the body).

As you work through each chakra, you may repeat a decree such as: "I AM the Violet Flame, clearing and balancing my chakras and restoring perfect health to my body." This practice helps to ensure that the energy is flowing freely through your body's energy centers, supporting physical, emotional, and spiritual well-being.

In addition to cleansing and balancing, the Violet Flame can be used to regenerate and revitalize the body's cells, promoting long-term health and vitality. This process involves not only clearing away toxins but also activating the body's natural healing mechanisms, which can lead to physical rejuvenation and the reversal of aging at the cellular level. The energy of the Violet Flame, when consistently applied, helps to renew the body's cells, allowing for greater longevity and physical resilience.

To work with the Violet Flame for regeneration, visualize the flame surrounding your entire body, but this time focus specifically on the cells. See the Violet Flame moving into each cell, purifying it of any toxins or negative energy and activating its natural regenerative powers. As the flame works, imagine your cells becoming more vibrant, healthy, and filled with life-force energy. You might use a decree such as: "I AM the Violet Flame, regenerating every cell in my body and restoring youthful vitality and strength." Continue this process for several minutes, feeling the energy of renewal and rejuvenation flowing through your entire being.

This practice can be especially beneficial for those who are recovering from illness or injury, as it supports the body's ability to heal and regenerate itself. By consistently working with the Violet Flame, you create an environment within your body that is conducive to healing, allowing for greater physical resilience and vitality over time.

It's important to recognize that physical body transformation with the Violet Flame is a gradual process. While you may experience immediate relief or improvement, the deeper healing and regeneration of the body's cells takes time and consistency. The more you work with the Violet Flame, the more you will notice shifts in your physical health, energy levels, and overall sense of well-being. Over time, this practice can lead to lasting physical transformation, as the body becomes more aligned with the higher frequencies of divine energy.

Incorporating the Violet Flame into your daily self-care routine can help to maintain and enhance your physical health. This might include regular meditation sessions with the Violet Flame, specific healing work on any areas of the body that need attention, and the use of healing decrees to support your body's natural healing processes. By making the Violet Flame a consistent part of your physical health regimen, you ensure that your body remains in a state of balance and vitality, aligned with your highest potential for health and well-being.

Through the power of the Violet Flame, you can experience profound physical transformation, not only by cleansing and purifying the body but also by activating its natural regenerative powers. As you continue to work with this energy, you will find that your body becomes more resilient, vibrant, and aligned with the flow of divine light. This process of physical renewal is a key aspect of holistic healing, as it supports the integration of body, mind, and spirit into a state of harmony and health.

In this part, we will explore practical techniques for applying the Violet Flame to specific areas of the physical body to promote healing, rejuvenation, and transformation. These techniques focus on using the Violet Flame's purifying and regenerating power to address common health issues, restore vitality to weakened areas, and enhance the body's natural healing processes. By engaging with these practices regularly, you will develop a deeper understanding of how the Violet Flame works on the physical level and learn how to direct its energy for optimal health and well-being.

The first technique involves targeting specific areas of the body that are experiencing pain, discomfort, or illness. Whether it's chronic pain, injury, or a health condition that has been affecting your body, the Violet Flame can be directed to these areas to transmute the energetic blockages or toxins contributing to the problem. To begin, sit or lie down in a quiet space where you can focus on your healing work. Close your eyes and take a few deep breaths to relax and center yourself. Visualize a column of Violet Flame surrounding your entire body, bringing a sense of warmth, peace, and protection.

Once you feel centered, bring your awareness to the area of your body that needs healing. Let's say you are experiencing discomfort in your lower back. Focus on this area and visualize the Violet Flame descending directly into it. Imagine the flame surrounding the affected muscles, bones, and nerves, dissolving any blockages, tension, or negative energy that may be contributing to the pain. As the flame works, see it transforming these lower vibrations into pure light, allowing your body to release the discomfort and tension.

You may repeat a healing decree as you focus on this process, such as: "I AM the Violet Flame, transmuting all pain and discord in my lower back and restoring perfect health and balance." With each repetition, feel the energy of the Violet Flame working more deeply, clearing away layers of accumulated tension, stress, or toxins that may have built up over time. Continue this practice for several minutes, allowing the Violet Flame to work until you feel a sense of relief or lightness in the area.

This technique can be adapted for any part of the body. Whether you are dealing with headaches, joint pain, digestive issues, or respiratory problems, the process remains the same. Simply focus on the area that needs healing, visualize the Violet Flame working in that specific part of the body, and use a decree that aligns with your healing intention. Over time, as you consistently apply this technique, you may notice a reduction in symptoms, increased comfort, and a sense of overall well-being.

In addition to addressing specific areas of discomfort, the Violet Flame can also be used to revitalize the body's energy systems, particularly the chakras and meridians. These energy pathways play a crucial role in maintaining physical health, as they regulate the flow of energy throughout the body. When these pathways become blocked or imbalanced, it can lead to physical, emotional, or mental health issues. By working with the Violet Flame to clear and balance these energy centers, you help to restore the natural flow of energy, supporting the body's ability to heal and maintain health.

Start by focusing on the root chakra, located at the base of the spine. The root chakra governs the body's foundation and connection to the Earth, and when it is blocked or imbalanced, it can lead to issues related to the legs, bones, and lower back. Visualize the Violet Flame surrounding the root chakra, gently dissolving any blockages or stagnant energy. As the flame works, see the energy of the root chakra becoming brighter, more vibrant, and balanced, allowing energy to flow freely through this area.

You may repeat the decree: "I AM the Violet Flame, clearing and balancing my root chakra and restoring strength and stability to my body." As you repeat this decree, feel the energy of the Violet Flame activating and harmonizing the root chakra, bringing a sense of grounding and physical strength. Once you feel the root chakra is balanced, move upward to the sacral chakra, which governs the reproductive organs and digestive system. Use the same process to clear and balance this chakra, visualizing the Violet Flame working through the lower abdomen and pelvis, restoring vitality to these areas.

Continue this practice for each of the chakras, moving up through the solar plexus, heart, throat, third eye, and crown chakras. As you work with the Violet Flame to balance and clear these energy centers, you are not only supporting your physical health but also promoting emotional and mental well-being. The alignment of the chakras ensures that energy flows smoothly throughout the body, helping to prevent illness and restore balance to any areas that may be affected by blockages or imbalances.

Another technique involves combining the Violet Flame with breathwork to enhance the healing process. Breath is a powerful tool for moving energy through the body, and when combined with the Violet Flame, it amplifies the purifying and regenerative effects. Begin by sitting in a comfortable position and focusing on your breath. Take slow, deep breaths, inhaling through the nose and exhaling through the mouth. With each inhale, visualize yourself breathing in the energy of the Violet Flame, filling your lungs and body with its purifying light.

As you exhale, imagine releasing any negative energy, toxins, or blockages from your body. See the Violet Flame burning away these lower vibrations as they leave your body with each breath. You can enhance this process by using a simple decree, such as: "With each breath, I AM the Violet Flame, transmuting all toxins and restoring perfect health to my body." Continue this breathwork for several minutes, feeling the energy of the Violet Flame circulating through your body, cleansing and renewing every cell.

This technique is particularly effective for releasing stress and tension that may accumulate in the body due to daily pressures or unresolved emotions. By incorporating breathwork with the Violet Flame, you create a powerful synergy that not only clears away negative energy but also revitalizes the body's systems, leaving you feeling lighter, more energized, and at peace.

In addition to these techniques, the Violet Flame can also be combined with the use of crystals to enhance its healing effects. Certain crystals, such as amethyst, are closely aligned with the energy of the Violet Flame and can act as amplifiers for its transformative power. To use crystals in your healing work, you can place them on or near the area of the body that needs healing, or you can hold them in your hands as you meditate with the Violet Flame.

For example, if you are working on healing a specific part of the body, such as the heart or lungs, you can place a crystal on your chest while you visualize the Violet Flame working in that area. As the Violet Flame flows through the crystal, its energy is magnified, allowing for deeper and more effective healing. You might also use a decree such as: "I AM the Violet Flame, working through this crystal to heal and restore my [specific area], filling it with divine light and vitality." The combination of the Violet Flame and the crystal's energy helps to accelerate the healing process, bringing greater balance and harmony to the body.

Another important practice for physical body transformation is consistency. While one session with the Violet Flame may bring immediate relief or improvement, long-term healing and transformation require regular practice. Make a habit of working with the Violet Flame daily, even if it's just for a few minutes at a time. Over time, this consistent application will lead to more profound shifts in your physical health, as well as in your emotional and spiritual well-being.

You can also incorporate the Violet Flame into your morning or evening routine to maintain physical balance and prevent illness. For example, each morning, you might spend a few minutes visualizing the Violet Flame surrounding your body and energizing your cells for the day ahead. Or, in the evening, you might use the Violet Flame to clear away any stress or tension from the day, allowing your body to rest and rejuvenate during sleep.

By consistently working with the Violet Flame, you are not only addressing current health issues but also strengthening your body's natural defenses against future imbalances. The transformative power of the Violet Flame creates a foundation for long-term physical health and resilience, allowing you to live with greater energy, vitality, and well-being.

The Violet Flame's ability to transmute lower energies, clear blockages, and promote regeneration makes it a powerful tool for physical body transformation. Whether you are using it to address specific health issues, balance your energy centers, or revitalize your entire body, the Violet Flame offers a direct and effective way to work with divine energy for healing. Through consistent practice, you can experience lasting physical transformation, supporting not only your body's health but also your overall spiritual growth and alignment with divine light.

Chapter 11
Crystals and the Violet Flame

Crystals are known for their ability to amplify, store, and transmit energy, and when combined with the Violet Flame, they become even more powerful tools for healing and transformation. Crystals can enhance the vibrational frequency of the Violet Flame, helping to direct its energy more precisely and effectively.

The vibrational qualities of crystals make them perfect companions in spiritual and energy work. Each crystal carries a unique frequency that can be used to promote healing, emotional balance, mental clarity, and spiritual growth. When you pair crystals with the Violet Flame, their natural frequencies align with the transformative energy of the flame, creating a powerful synergy that enhances the healing process. Crystals can absorb and transmit the energy of the Violet Flame into your body, energy field, or environment, amplifying its effects and promoting deeper levels of healing.

The most closely aligned crystal with the Violet Flame is amethyst, a purple or violet-colored quartz that is revered for its ability to transmute negative energy, calm the mind, and promote spiritual awakening. Amethyst carries the same high-frequency energy as the Violet Flame, making it an ideal tool for working with this spiritual fire. Amethyst can be used in personal healing, meditation, or space clearing, helping to transmute lower vibrations and replace them with the pure, uplifting energy of the Violet Flame.

To begin working with amethyst in combination with the Violet Flame, start by selecting an amethyst crystal that resonates with you. The crystal can be a small stone, a cluster, or even an amethyst geode—what matters is that you feel a connection with it. Before using the crystal, it is important to cleanse it of any unwanted energies. You can cleanse your crystal by holding it under running water for a few minutes, leaving it in the moonlight overnight, or using the Violet Flame to purify it energetically. To cleanse your crystal with the Violet Flame, hold the amethyst in your hands and visualize the Violet Flame surrounding it, dissolving any lower vibrations or energies that may have accumulated in the stone.

Once your crystal is cleansed, you can use it in a variety of ways to amplify the Violet Flame's healing energy. One simple method is to hold the amethyst in your hands while you meditate on the Violet Flame. Sit in a comfortable position, close your eyes, and take a few deep breaths to center yourself. Hold the amethyst in your dominant hand (the hand through which you most easily send energy) and visualize the Violet Flame surrounding your entire body. As you hold the crystal, feel its energy merging with the Violet Flame, amplifying its purifying and healing effects.

As you focus on the combined energy of the amethyst and the Violet Flame, you may repeat a decree such as: "I AM the Violet Flame, transmuting all negative energies within and around me, amplified by the power of amethyst." As you repeat this decree, feel the energy of the Violet Flame working more deeply through your body and energy field, dissolving any negative energies or blockages and replacing them with pure light. The amethyst acts as a conduit for the Violet Flame's energy, helping to direct it where it is most needed.

Another powerful way to use amethyst with the Violet Flame is to place the crystal directly on areas of your body that need healing. For example, if you are experiencing tension or pain in a specific part of your body, place the amethyst on that area while visualizing the Violet Flame surrounding it. See the Violet Flame and the crystal's energy working together to dissolve any tension, pain, or blockages, restoring balance and health to the area. You may repeat a healing decree such as: "I AM the Violet Flame, amplified by amethyst, transmuting all pain and restoring perfect health to this area."

In addition to amethyst, there are several other crystals that resonate strongly with the energy of the Violet Flame and can be used to support healing and transformation. One such crystal is sugilite, a deep purple stone known for its ability to protect against negative energy, promote spiritual alignment, and encourage emotional healing. Sugilite is particularly effective in clearing emotional blockages and helping to release patterns of fear, guilt, and self-doubt. When combined with the Violet Flame, sugilite enhances the energy of emotional healing, making it an excellent crystal for transmuting emotional wounds.

To use sugilite with the Violet Flame, hold the stone in your hands and focus on a specific emotional issue you would like to heal. Visualize the Violet Flame surrounding your heart center, where emotional energy is stored, and see the sugilite amplifying the energy of the flame. As the Violet Flame and the sugilite work together, imagine the flame dissolving any emotional pain or blockages, allowing you to release old patterns and emotional wounds. You may repeat a decree such as: "I AM the Violet Flame, with the power of sugilite, healing all emotional wounds and restoring peace to my heart."

Another crystal that works well with the Violet Flame is fluorite, particularly purple fluorite. Fluorite is known for its ability to cleanse and stabilize the aura, remove negative energies, and enhance mental clarity. Purple fluorite, in particular, resonates with the energy of the Violet Flame and can be used to transmute mental patterns that no longer serve you, such as negative thinking, confusion, or self-limiting beliefs. When paired with the Violet Flame, fluorite helps to clear the mind and bring in a sense of clarity and focus.

To use fluorite with the Violet Flame for mental clarity, hold a piece of purple fluorite in your hands or place it on your forehead, where the third eye chakra is located. Visualize the Violet Flame surrounding your mind, dissolving any mental clutter, confusion, or negative thought patterns. As the flame works, see the fluorite amplifying this energy, helping you to release any thoughts or beliefs that are no longer aligned with your highest good. You may use a decree such as: "I AM the Violet Flame, amplified by fluorite, clearing my mind of all confusion and bringing in divine clarity and focus."

Lepidolite, a lilac-colored crystal rich in lithium, is another excellent crystal to combine with the Violet Flame, especially for those dealing with stress, anxiety, or insomnia. Lepidolite's soothing energy helps to calm the mind and body, making it an ideal crystal for promoting relaxation and emotional balance. When paired with the Violet Flame, lepidolite can help to transmute anxiety, stress, and emotional turbulence, allowing you to feel more peaceful and centered.

To work with lepidolite and the Violet Flame, hold the crystal in your hands before bed or during moments of stress. Visualize the Violet Flame surrounding your entire body, calming and soothing your energy. See the lepidolite amplifying the energy of the Violet Flame, helping to transmute any anxiety or stress you may be carrying. You may repeat a decree such as: "I AM the Violet Flame, with the power of lepidolite, transmuting all stress and anxiety and restoring peace to my mind and body." As you repeat this decree, feel the combined energies of the Violet Flame and lepidolite bringing a sense of calm and serenity to your entire being.

Crystals can also be used in combination with the Violet Flame for space clearing and protection. Just as crystals can be placed on the body to amplify healing, they can also be placed in a room or living space to enhance the energy of the environment. To clear a space with the Violet Flame and crystals, place amethyst, fluorite, or another Violet Flame-aligned crystal in the center of the room. Visualize the Violet Flame filling the room, transmuting any negative or stagnant energy. As the Violet Flame works, see the crystal amplifying its energy, helping to cleanse and uplift the space.

You may use a space-clearing decree such as: "I AM the Violet Flame, with the power of these crystals, clearing and protecting this space from all negative energies." As you repeat this decree, feel the energy in the room becoming lighter, more harmonious, and filled with divine light. This practice can be done regularly to maintain a high vibration in your home, workspace, or any environment where you spend time.

By incorporating crystals into your Violet Flame practice, you enhance the power of this transformative energy, allowing for deeper healing and more profound spiritual growth. Whether you are using amethyst, sugilite, fluorite, or lepidolite, each crystal brings its unique energy to the process, helping to amplify the Violet Flame's ability to transmute negative energies, clear blockages, and restore balance. As you continue to work with these powerful tools, you will experience greater levels of healing, clarity, and spiritual alignment, both in your personal energy and in the environments around you.

One of the most effective ways to harness the combined energy of the Violet Flame and crystals is through the creation of a crystal grid. A crystal grid is an arrangement of crystals that work together to amplify the energy being directed toward a particular intention. When set up correctly, the grid acts as a magnifier, channeling the energy of the Violet Flame more intensely to promote healing, protection, or transformation. Crystal grids can be used for personal healing, space clearing, or even for sending healing energy to others.

To create a crystal grid with the Violet Flame, start by selecting a location where the grid will not be disturbed, such as a meditation space, altar, or a quiet corner of your home. The grid's layout will depend on the specific intention, but a common shape for a healing grid is a circle, symbolizing wholeness and protection. You will need several crystals to form the grid. Amethyst, clear quartz, fluorite, and other Violet Flame-aligned stones are excellent choices. Clear quartz is particularly useful because it can amplify the energy of any other crystal it is paired with, making it a versatile stone for grids.

Begin by placing a larger central crystal, ideally amethyst, in the middle of the grid. This central crystal will act as the anchor for the energy of the grid. Around this central crystal, place smaller stones in a circular or geometric pattern, depending on the shape of the grid. For example, you might use four crystals placed in the cardinal directions (north, south, east, and west), or create a star-shaped grid with six or eight points. The number of crystals and the layout will depend on your intuitive guidance and the specific goal of the grid.

Once the stones are arranged, take a few moments to focus on your intention for the grid. This might be for physical healing, emotional balance, protection, or even spiritual transformation. As you hold this intention, visualize the Violet Flame surrounding the entire grid, filling it with its transformative energy. You can enhance this visualization by repeating a decree such as: "I AM the Violet Flame, amplifying the healing power of these crystals, restoring perfect health and harmony." As you repeat the decree, see the energy of the Violet Flame moving through the central crystal and spreading out to the surrounding stones, creating a powerful flow of healing energy.

After setting the intention and activating the grid, you can leave it in place to continue working for as long as needed. Crystal grids work over time, so you may wish to keep the grid in place for several days, weeks, or until the healing process feels complete. You can revisit the grid daily to recharge it by repeating your intention and visualizing the Violet Flame continuing to amplify the energy of the crystals.

Another practical application of crystals and the Violet Flame is through the use of healing rituals. Rituals provide a structured way to focus your energy and intentions, making them particularly effective for working with the combined energies of the Violet Flame and crystals. A healing ritual using the Violet Flame and crystals can be performed for yourself, others, or even for planetary healing.

To begin a healing ritual, gather the crystals that align with the specific type of healing you wish to perform. For example, if you are focusing on emotional healing, you might choose amethyst and rose quartz, both of which resonate with the heart and emotional balance. If your intention is physical healing, you might use clear quartz, green aventurine, or amethyst for their restorative and amplifying properties.

Set up a small altar or space where you can place the crystals. Light a candle or incense if you wish to create a peaceful atmosphere. Hold the central crystal in your hands and focus on your intention for the healing ritual. You may say a prayer or an affirmation, such as: "I call upon the energy of the Violet Flame and these crystals to assist in the healing of [your name or the name of the person you are healing]. I ask for the energy to be directed where it is most needed, restoring perfect health, peace, and balance."

As you set your intention, visualize the Violet Flame surrounding the crystals and the space where you are working. See the energy of the flame and the crystals merging together, creating a powerful flow of healing light. You may wish to repeat a decree such as: "I AM the Violet Flame, working with the energy of these crystals to transmute all negative energies and restore divine balance." As you repeat the decree, feel the energy building and expanding, creating a healing vortex around you or the person you are sending healing to.

Once the energy feels strong, place the crystals on your body or direct the energy toward the recipient. If you are working on yourself, you can place the crystals on specific energy centers or areas that need healing, such as the heart, solar plexus, or third eye. If you are working on someone else, visualize the Violet Flame and crystal energy flowing to them, surrounding their body and energy field with healing light. Continue this process for several minutes, allowing the energy to flow naturally. When you feel the healing is complete, give thanks to the Violet Flame and the crystals for their assistance.

In addition to rituals and grids, you can also incorporate crystals and the Violet Flame into your daily meditation practice. By meditating with a crystal that resonates with the Violet Flame, you can enhance the healing and spiritual alignment that comes from working with this transformative energy. Begin by holding a crystal, such as amethyst or fluorite, in your hand as you meditate.

Visualize the Violet Flame surrounding both you and the crystal, amplifying the crystal's natural frequency and guiding its energy toward healing or transformation.

As you meditate, focus on a specific healing intention, whether it's physical, emotional, or spiritual. Let the combined energy of the crystal and the Violet Flame work together to transmute any blockages or imbalances, filling you with light and clarity. You may repeat a simple affirmation such as: "I AM the Violet Flame, working with this crystal to heal, transform, and restore balance to my body, mind, and spirit." This meditation practice can be done regularly to maintain energetic balance and enhance your connection to the transformative power of the Violet Flame.

Another powerful use of crystals and the Violet Flame is for distance healing. If someone you care about is in need of healing but is not physically present, you can use a crystal in combination with the Violet Flame to send healing energy across distances. To do this, hold the crystal in your hands and focus on the person you wish to send healing to. You may choose to hold a photograph of the person or visualize them clearly in your mind.

As you hold the crystal, visualize the Violet Flame surrounding the person, dissolving any negative energies or blockages. See the crystal's energy amplifying the healing power of the Violet Flame, directing it to the areas where the person needs healing. You can repeat a decree such as: "I AM the Violet Flame, amplified by this crystal, sending healing and light to [person's name], restoring them to divine balance and harmony." Continue to hold this visualization for several minutes, trusting that the energy is being received by the person, no matter how far away they are.

For those who wish to work on space clearing and protection, combining crystals with the Violet Flame offers a practical way to keep your environment energetically clean and harmonious. Place crystals such as amethyst or clear quartz in key areas of your home, such as near doors, windows, or in the center of rooms. Visualize the Violet Flame working through the crystals, purifying the space and transmuting any negative or stagnant energy. You can reinforce this process by using a decree like: "I AM the Violet Flame, working with these crystals to cleanse and protect this space from all lower vibrations."

In summary, the practical applications of crystals and the Violet Flame in healing are vast and powerful. Whether you are creating crystal grids, performing healing rituals, meditating, or sending distance healing, the combination of these two energies enhances your ability to transmute negative energies, restore balance, and promote physical, emotional, and spiritual well-being. Through consistent practice, you will develop a deeper connection to the crystals you work with and the transformative power of the Violet Flame, leading to profound healing and growth in your life and the lives of those you care for.

Chapter 12
Energy Protection for the Healer

For anyone practicing healing—whether on themselves or others—energy protection is essential. As a healer, you open yourself to various energetic influences during your work, and without proper protection, these energies can affect your own well-being.

When you engage in healing work, whether it's for yourself, others, or the planet, your energy field expands to accommodate the flow of healing energy. This expansion can make you more sensitive to external influences, including the emotions, thoughts, and energies of those around you. While this sensitivity is useful for tuning into others' needs, it also leaves you more vulnerable to absorbing negative or discordant energies. If you do not actively protect your energy field, you might find yourself feeling drained, anxious, or emotionally unbalanced after healing sessions.

The first step in energy protection is understanding that your energy field, or aura, functions as your natural shield. The aura surrounds your physical body and serves as a barrier between you and external energies. However, this barrier can weaken or become permeable over time, especially if you're exposed to intense emotional or energetic exchanges during healing. Strengthening your aura and keeping it clear are vital to maintaining your energetic health. The Violet Flame, along with other Sacred Flames, is a powerful tool for purifying and fortifying your aura, ensuring that your energy remains protected and resilient.

To begin protecting your energy, start by establishing a daily practice of cleansing and strengthening your aura. This practice can be done at the start of each day to prepare yourself for any healing work or energetic exchanges you may encounter. Sit or stand in a quiet space, close your eyes, and take a few deep breaths to center yourself. Visualize the Violet Flame surrounding your entire body, forming a sphere of light that extends about three feet around you in all directions. See this sphere of Violet Flame as your protective shield, burning away any negative or unwanted energies that may try to enter your space.

As you hold this visualization, repeat a decree for protection, such as: "I AM the Violet Flame, surrounding and protecting my energy field from all external influences." As you repeat this decree, feel the energy of the Violet Flame intensifying, creating a strong, impenetrable shield around you. This shield will not only protect you from absorbing negative energies but will also help transmute any lower vibrations you may encounter throughout the day. You can reinforce this practice by repeating the visualization and decree before and after any healing session or interaction that requires heightened energetic protection.

In addition to using the Violet Flame, the Blue Flame of protection is another powerful energy for safeguarding your aura. The Blue Flame, associated with Archangel Michael, carries the qualities of divine protection, strength, and resilience. You can invoke the Blue Flame to fortify your aura even further, creating a multi-layered shield that protects you from psychic attacks, emotional overwhelm, and energetic depletion.

To work with the Blue Flame, visualize a vibrant blue light surrounding the outer edge of your Violet Flame shield. See this blue light forming a second layer of protection around your body, adding an extra level of strength and security. As you visualize the Blue Flame, repeat the decree: "I AM the Blue Flame of protection, shielding my energy from all lower vibrations and influences." This combined shield of the Violet Flame and Blue Flame creates a powerful energetic barrier, ensuring that you remain protected and grounded during any healing work or interaction.

In addition to fortifying your aura, it's important to clear your energy field after each healing session. During healing, you may unknowingly absorb the emotions, thoughts, or energetic blockages of the person you are working with. If these energies are not cleared from your field, they can linger and affect your mood, health, and energy levels. After each healing session, take a few moments to purify your energy and release any unwanted influences.

To do this, visualize the Violet Flame surrounding your entire body once again, but this time, focus on the flame actively clearing away any residual energy that does not belong to you. See the Violet Flame dissolving any emotional or energetic cords that may have formed during the session, allowing them to be transmuted into light. You may repeat the decree: "I AM the Violet Flame, clearing and transmuting all energies from this healing session, restoring my energy to its highest vibration." This practice ensures that you remain energetically clear and balanced, preventing you from carrying the energetic burdens of others.

Another essential aspect of energy protection is setting clear energetic boundaries before beginning any healing work. Boundaries are not only physical but also energetic, and they help define where your energy ends and another's begins. By setting intentional boundaries, you prevent the merging or entanglement of your energy with that of the person you are healing. This practice helps you stay grounded and prevents emotional overwhelm or energetic drain.

Before starting a healing session, take a few moments to center yourself and visualize your energetic boundary. You can imagine this boundary as a layer of light or a shield that surrounds your body, indicating the space within which your energy is contained. As you visualize this boundary, set the intention that while you will be open to channeling healing energy, your personal energy will remain protected and separate from the energy of the person you are working with. You might say a simple affirmation, such as: "I set clear energetic boundaries, remaining fully protected as I offer healing energy." This boundary-setting practice reinforces your energetic integrity and ensures that you maintain your strength and clarity throughout the session.

For healers who work frequently with others, grounding is another crucial practice for maintaining energy protection. Grounding helps to anchor your energy in the Earth, ensuring that you remain stable, centered, and connected to your physical body. When you are grounded, you are less likely to be affected by the fluctuating emotions or energies of those around you. Grounding also helps to discharge any excess energy you may pick up during healing sessions, preventing you from feeling scattered or unbalanced.

To ground yourself, stand or sit with your feet flat on the floor and take a few deep breaths. Visualize roots extending from the soles of your feet, going deep into the Earth. As the roots grow, feel your connection to the Earth becoming stronger, anchoring you firmly in the present moment. You may also visualize the energy of the Earth rising up through your feet, filling your body with stabilizing, grounding energy. Repeat a grounding affirmation such as: "I AM grounded and fully present, connected to the Earth and protected by divine light." Grounding exercises can be done before, during, and after healing sessions to ensure that your energy remains stable and centered.

In addition to these personal practices, it's important to maintain the energetic cleanliness of your healing space. Just as your aura can absorb external energies, so can the spaces in which you work. If you frequently conduct healing sessions in the same room or environment, the space can accumulate residual energies that may affect your work or your clients. Regularly clearing and protecting your healing space ensures that it remains a high-vibrational environment, free from stagnant or negative energies.

To clear your healing space, use the Violet Flame in combination with crystals or other tools such as sage or sound healing instruments. Begin by visualizing the Violet Flame filling the entire space, transmuting any negative or stagnant energy. As the flame moves through the room, see it dissolving any energetic imprints from previous sessions, clearing the space of all lower vibrations. You may repeat a decree such as: "I AM the Violet Flame, purifying this space and restoring it to divine harmony." You can also place amethyst or clear quartz crystals in the corners of the room to maintain a high vibration and amplify the protective energy.

In some cases, you may also encounter energetic attachments or cords during healing sessions, particularly if you are working with individuals who are dealing with strong emotional issues, traumas, or negative thought patterns. These cords can form between you and the person you are healing, draining your energy and creating an unwanted energetic link. To protect yourself from energetic attachments, it's important to sever any cords after each session.

To cut energetic cords, visualize the Violet Flame surrounding your body and dissolving any cords or attachments that may have formed during the session. You may also call upon Archangel Michael and the Blue Flame of protection to assist in cutting these cords. As you focus on releasing the attachments, repeat a decree such as: "I AM the Violet Flame, dissolving all cords and attachments, restoring my energy to wholeness." This practice ensures that you remain energetically free and unattached after each session, preventing emotional or energetic drain.

By incorporating these energy protection practices into your healing work, you will not only safeguard your own well-being but also enhance your ability to offer effective, clear, and compassionate healing to others. Protection is an essential part of being a healer, as it allows you to maintain your energetic integrity and avoid burnout or emotional overwhelm. As you continue to strengthen your energy field and apply these techniques, you will become more confident in your ability to navigate the energetic dynamics of healing, knowing that you are fully protected and supported by the divine.

Having established the importance of maintaining a strong energetic field and creating clear boundaries, this part focuses on practical techniques to deepen energy protection for healers. These methods include working with advanced visualization techniques, using decrees more effectively, and employing tools such as crystals, essential oils, and sound healing to enhance your energetic defenses. By incorporating these practices into your daily routine, you will fortify your ability to work as a healer without absorbing unwanted energies or experiencing burnout.

One powerful technique for protecting your energy is layered shielding, which involves creating multiple protective layers around your aura. Each layer serves a different function, offering protection against various types of energetic interference. Layered shielding is especially useful for healers who work with clients regularly or deal with emotionally intense or complex energy dynamics.

To begin, visualize your aura as a series of concentric spheres surrounding your body. Start with the inner layer, which is closest to your physical body, and visualize it as a bright, glowing light. This layer is your personal space, where your energy is most concentrated. Use the Violet Flame to cleanse and strengthen this inner layer by visualizing the flame moving through it, transmuting any negative energies. Repeat a decree such as: "I AM the Violet Flame, clearing and fortifying my personal energy field."

Next, visualize the second layer of your shield, which surrounds your aura at a distance of about three feet. This layer serves as a barrier against external influences, including the energies of other people and the environment. Visualize this layer as a brilliant blue light, the energy of the Blue Flame of protection. See this light forming a solid, impenetrable shield around your body. As you visualize this protective layer, repeat the decree: "I AM the Blue Flame, shielding my energy from all external vibrations and influences."

The final, outermost layer of your shield can be visualized as a golden or white light. This layer represents divine protection and connection to the higher realms, ensuring that you remain aligned with your highest spiritual purpose while protected from lower vibrational energies. As you visualize this outer layer, imagine it radiating pure light and reflecting any negative or discordant energies away from you. Use a decree such as: "I AM protected by divine light, surrounded by peace and harmony, aligned with my highest self." This three-layered shield can be activated at the start of each day or before any healing session, offering comprehensive protection for your energy field.

Another technique for energy protection is mirroring, where you visualize a reflective surface around your aura that reflects negative energy back to its source without absorbing it. This method is especially useful for healers who work in environments where they are exposed to many different types of energy, such as hospitals, therapy centers, or large gatherings. To create a mirror shield, visualize a reflective, silver surface surrounding your aura. This surface acts like a mirror, allowing you to remain open to positive energies while reflecting negative or harmful energies away from you.

As you visualize this mirror shield, repeat the decree: "I AM surrounded by a mirror of divine light, reflecting all negativity away from me and retaining only the highest vibrations." This practice ensures that you can engage with others' energy without becoming entangled in it, allowing you to offer healing from a place of strength and clarity.

Crystals are powerful allies for energy protection, as they carry specific vibrational frequencies that can enhance your natural shields and transmute negative energy. Several crystals are particularly effective for protection, including black tourmaline, smoky quartz, and labradorite. These stones help to absorb or deflect negative energies, making them ideal companions for healers who wish to remain energetically clear during their work.

To use black tourmaline for protection, place the stone in your healing space or carry it with you during sessions. Visualize the black tourmaline absorbing any negative energies that may arise during the session, preventing them from entering your aura. You may also place the stone near your feet to help ground and stabilize your energy while you work. Repeat a decree such as: "I AM protected by the energy of black tourmaline, grounding my energy and transmuting all negativity."

Smoky quartz is another powerful protective stone that helps to neutralize negative vibrations and ground excess energy. Like black tourmaline, smoky quartz can be placed in your healing space or carried with you during sessions. To enhance its protective qualities, you can program the stone with an intention by holding it in your hands and visualizing it being filled with the Violet Flame. As you set this intention, repeat a decree such as: "I AM the Violet Flame, working through this smoky quartz to transmute all lower energies and restore balance."

Labradorite is a protective stone known for its ability to shield the aura from unwanted energies while promoting clarity and insight. It is especially useful for healers who are sensitive to the emotions and thoughts of others. Labradorite can be worn as jewelry or placed in your healing space to enhance your energetic boundaries. To use labradorite for protection, hold the stone in your hands and visualize it forming a protective barrier around your aura. Repeat the decree: "I AM protected by the energy of labradorite, shielding my aura from all external influences."

Essential oils are another valuable tool for enhancing energy protection. Certain oils, such as frankincense, myrrh, and lavender, carry protective and purifying properties that can help strengthen your energy field. To use essential oils for protection, you can diffuse them in your healing space, apply them to your body, or create a protective spray by mixing a few drops of oil with water in a spray bottle.

Frankincense is particularly effective for raising your vibration and creating a protective barrier around your energy. Before a healing session, apply a drop of frankincense oil to your wrists, neck, or the soles of your feet. As you apply the oil, visualize the Violet Flame surrounding you, creating a shield of light that protects you from lower energies. Repeat the decree: "I AM surrounded by divine protection, my energy field is clear and fortified by the energy of frankincense."

Lavender oil is known for its calming and balancing properties, making it an excellent choice for healers who wish to remain emotionally centered during their work. To use lavender for protection, diffuse it in your healing space or apply a few drops to your temples before a session. As you inhale the soothing scent of lavender, visualize your energy field being cleansed and stabilized. Repeat the decree: "I AM the energy of peace and balance, protected and guided by divine light."

Sound healing is another effective method for maintaining energy protection. The vibration of sound helps to clear and stabilize your aura, removing any residual energies that may have attached to you during healing sessions. Instruments such as singing bowls, tuning forks, and chimes are excellent tools for this purpose, as their sound waves penetrate the energy field and break up stagnant or discordant energies.

To use sound for protection, you can play a singing bowl or tuning fork around your body after a healing session, allowing the sound to cleanse and realign your energy. As the sound vibrates through your aura, visualize the Violet Flame dissolving any negative energies and restoring your field to its natural state of balance. Repeat a decree such as: "I AM the Violet Flame, transmuting all energies with the power of sound, restoring harmony and protection to my aura."

In addition to personal protection, it is also important to protect your healing space from energetic interference. After each healing session, clear the space of any lingering energies by using the Violet Flame, crystals, essential oils, or sound. Start by visualizing the Violet Flame filling the room, burning away any residual energy from the session. You can also use sound, such as a bell or chime, to clear the space. As you clear the room, repeat a decree such as: "I AM the Violet Flame, clearing this space and restoring it to divine harmony and protection."

You may also place protective crystals such as amethyst, black tourmaline, or clear quartz in the corners of the room to maintain a high vibration and prevent the accumulation of lower energies. Essential oils like sage or palo santo can be diffused to purify the space, while repeating a decree like: "I AM the divine energy of purity and protection, creating a sacred space for healing."

By consistently applying these techniques for energy protection, you ensure that your energy field remains strong, clear, and resilient, no matter how often you engage in healing work. Protection is not just about shielding yourself from negative energies—it is about maintaining your alignment with divine light and ensuring that you can offer healing from a place of strength and clarity. As you incorporate these practices into your daily routine, you will feel more confident and empowered in your role as a healer, knowing that your energy is fully protected and supported by the divine.

Chapter 13
Balancing the Chakras with the Energy of Saint Germain

The chakra system is an essential aspect of our energetic health, influencing both physical and spiritual well-being. Chakras are energy centers within the body, each corresponding to different aspects of life, such as survival, creativity, emotional balance, and spiritual insight. When our chakras are in balance, we experience harmony in all areas of life. However, when one or more chakras are blocked or overactive, it can lead to physical discomfort, emotional challenges, or spiritual stagnation. Saint Germain's teachings, particularly through the use of the Violet Flame, offer powerful methods for balancing the chakras, restoring alignment, and raising your energetic frequency.

The energy of Saint Germain is particularly attuned to the higher chakras, such as the third eye and crown, as his teachings focus on spiritual awakening, transformation, and connection to divine wisdom. However, all chakras must be in balance for the body, mind, and spirit to function in harmony. The Violet Flame, with its purifying and transmuting properties, can be used to cleanse and activate each chakra, dissolving any blockages and restoring the natural flow of energy throughout the body.

To begin working with the chakras, it's important to understand the basic function of each energy center. There are seven main chakras, each located along the spine from the base to the crown of the head. Starting from the bottom, the root chakra, located at the base of the spine, governs our sense of safety, stability, and physical survival. When the root chakra is balanced, we feel grounded and secure. The sacral chakra, located just below the navel, is associated with creativity, emotions, and sexual energy. A balanced sacral chakra allows for healthy emotional expression and creative flow.

The solar plexus chakra, located in the upper abdomen, governs personal power, confidence, and willpower. When this chakra is balanced, we feel empowered and capable of achieving our goals. The heart chakra, located in the center of the chest, is the seat of love, compassion, and connection. A balanced heart chakra allows us to give and receive love freely, with a sense of inner peace. The throat chakra, located at the base of the throat, governs communication, truth, and self-expression. When in balance, this chakra allows us to express ourselves authentically and with clarity.

The third eye chakra, located between the eyebrows, is associated with intuition, insight, and spiritual awareness. A balanced third eye chakra enhances our ability to perceive beyond the physical realm and connect with higher wisdom. Finally, the crown chakra, located at the top of the head, is our connection to the divine and the higher self. When the crown chakra is open and balanced, we experience a sense of unity with the universe and a deep connection to spiritual truth.

To begin balancing the chakras with the energy of Saint Germain and the Violet Flame, find a quiet space where you can sit comfortably and undisturbed. Close your eyes and take a few deep breaths, allowing yourself to relax and center your awareness. Visualize a column of Violet Flame descending from above, surrounding your entire body. See this flame gently cleansing your energy field, preparing you to work with the chakras.

Start with the root chakra, located at the base of the spine. Visualize a spinning wheel of red light at this chakra, representing the energy of grounding and stability. As you hold this visualization, see the Violet Flame surrounding the red light, purifying any blockages or stagnant energy. You may repeat a decree such as: "I AM the Violet Flame, clearing and balancing my root chakra, restoring perfect stability and grounding." As you repeat the decree, feel the energy of the root chakra becoming more vibrant and balanced, anchoring you firmly to the Earth.

Next, move your awareness to the sacral chakra, located just below the navel. Visualize this chakra as a spinning wheel of orange light, representing creativity and emotional flow. See the Violet Flame surrounding this orange light, dissolving any blockages related to emotional pain, creative stagnation, or unresolved feelings. Repeat the decree: "I AM the Violet Flame, clearing and balancing my sacral chakra, restoring perfect creativity and emotional harmony." Feel the energy of the sacral chakra becoming clearer and more balanced, allowing for healthy emotional expression and creative flow.

Continue upward to the solar plexus chakra, located in the upper abdomen. Visualize this chakra as a spinning wheel of yellow light, representing personal power and confidence. As the Violet Flame surrounds this yellow light, imagine it dissolving any blockages related to self-doubt, fear, or lack of willpower. Repeat the decree: "I AM the Violet Flame, clearing and balancing my solar plexus chakra, restoring perfect confidence and personal power." As you repeat the decree, feel the energy of the solar plexus chakra becoming stronger and more balanced, empowering you to take action and move forward with confidence.

Next, bring your awareness to the heart chakra, located in the center of the chest. Visualize a spinning wheel of green or pink light at this chakra, representing love, compassion, and connection. As the Violet Flame surrounds this light, see it dissolving any blockages related to grief, fear of vulnerability, or emotional pain. Repeat the decree: "I AM the Violet Flame, clearing and balancing my heart chakra, restoring perfect love and compassion." As you repeat the decree, feel the energy of the heart chakra expanding, filling you with a sense of peace, love, and connection to yourself and others.

Move your awareness up to the throat chakra, located at the base of the throat. Visualize a spinning wheel of blue light at this chakra, representing communication and truth. As the Violet

Flame surrounds this blue light, see it dissolving any blockages related to fear of self-expression, dishonesty, or suppressed emotions. Repeat the decree: "I AM the Violet Flame, clearing and balancing my throat chakra, restoring perfect communication and self-expression." As you repeat the decree, feel the energy of the throat chakra becoming clearer, allowing you to express yourself authentically and speak your truth with confidence.

Next, focus on the third eye chakra, located between the eyebrows. Visualize this chakra as a spinning wheel of indigo light, representing intuition and spiritual insight. As the Violet Flame surrounds this indigo light, see it dissolving any blockages related to confusion, doubt, or lack of clarity. Repeat the decree: "I AM the Violet Flame, clearing and balancing my third eye chakra, restoring perfect intuition and spiritual vision." As you repeat the decree, feel the energy of the third eye chakra expanding, enhancing your intuitive abilities and connection to higher wisdom.

Bring your awareness to the crown chakra, located at the top of the head. Visualize a spinning wheel of violet or white light at this chakra, representing your connection to the divine and the higher self. As the Violet Flame surrounds this light, see it dissolving any blockages related to disconnection from spirit, feelings of isolation, or lack of purpose. Repeat the decree: "I AM the Violet Flame, clearing and balancing my crown chakra, restoring perfect spiritual connection and divine alignment." As you repeat the decree, feel the energy of the crown chakra opening and expanding, allowing for a deeper connection to the divine and a sense of unity with the universe.

Once you have worked through all seven chakras, take a few moments to sit quietly and notice how your energy feels. You may feel lighter, more centered, and more aligned with your true self. Balancing the chakras with the Violet Flame helps to restore harmony to your energy field, supporting both physical and spiritual health. By regularly engaging in this practice, you can maintain the balance of your chakras and experience greater clarity, peace, and alignment in your daily life.

In addition to personal chakra work, you can also use this method to help others balance their chakras. Whether you are working with clients, friends, or family members, the process remains the same: visualize the Violet Flame surrounding each chakra, use decrees to invoke the energy, and guide the person through the process of clearing and balancing their energy centers. This practice can bring profound healing and transformation, helping others to align their energy with their highest potential.

As you continue to work with the Violet Flame and Saint Germain's energy, you will develop a deeper understanding of the chakra system and how it influences your overall well-being. The more balanced and aligned your chakras are, the more easily you can flow through life with grace, purpose, and spiritual clarity. This balance allows you to access the full spectrum of your potential, bringing harmony to your physical, emotional, mental, and spiritual bodies.

Now that you have learned how to work with the Violet Flame to clear and balance each of the seven chakras, it's time to focus on more advanced techniques that deepen this connection and allow for sustained alignment of the chakra system. These techniques will not only help to maintain balance but also activate and enhance the energy flow between the chakras, promoting a more integrated and powerful energetic system.

One advanced method for balancing the chakras is chakra alignment through breathwork. Breath is a powerful tool for moving energy through the body, and when combined with the Violet Flame, it can accelerate the clearing and alignment of the chakras. This practice involves focusing on the breath while consciously directing the Violet Flame to flow through each of the chakras, creating a continuous circuit of energy that harmonizes and activates the entire system.

To begin, sit in a comfortable position with your spine straight and your feet grounded on the floor. Close your eyes and take a few deep breaths to center yourself. Visualize a column of Violet Flame descending from above, moving down through your crown chakra and aligning along the spine, where the chakras are located. As you breathe in, imagine the Violet Flame flowing upward from the root chakra to the crown chakra, filling each energy center with purifying light. As you exhale, visualize the Violet Flame flowing downward from the crown to the root, clearing away any blockages and restoring balance.

With each inhale, focus on drawing the Violet Flame through the chakras, starting at the base of the spine and moving upward through the sacral, solar plexus, heart, throat, third eye, and crown chakras. As you exhale, imagine the energy flowing back down through the same path. This creates a circular flow of energy that continuously purifies and balances each chakra. Repeat this cycle for several minutes, allowing the breath to synchronize with the flow of the Violet Flame. You may use a decree such as: "I AM the Violet Flame, flowing through my chakras, balancing and harmonizing my entire energy system."

As you work with this breathwork technique, you will begin to feel a sense of lightness and alignment as the energy moves freely through your body. The continuous flow of the Violet Flame helps to keep the chakras open and balanced, preventing the buildup of stagnant energy and supporting overall energetic health.

In addition to breathwork, guided meditations can be a powerful tool for deepening your connection to the chakras and ensuring their alignment. Meditations that focus specifically on chakra activation allow you to connect more deeply with each energy center, bringing awareness to the qualities and characteristics associated with each one. These meditations can be done regularly to keep your chakras balanced and to cultivate a deeper sense of connection to your higher self.

To practice a guided chakra meditation with the Violet Flame, find a quiet space where you won't be disturbed. Begin by taking a few deep breaths to relax and center your awareness. Visualize the Violet Flame surrounding your body, creating a protective and purifying field of energy. Starting with the root chakra, bring your attention to the base of the spine and imagine a red sphere of light spinning there. As you focus on this energy center, visualize the Violet Flame entering the chakra, purifying and balancing it. You can repeat the decree: "I AM the Violet Flame, balancing my root chakra and restoring perfect stability."

Move your awareness to each chakra in sequence, visualizing the appropriate color and focusing on the energy center's qualities. At the sacral chakra, visualize orange and focus on creativity and emotional balance. For the solar plexus, visualize yellow and focus on personal power and confidence. At the heart chakra, visualize green or pink and focus on love and compassion. For the throat chakra, visualize blue and focus on communication and truth. At the third eye, visualize indigo and focus on intuition and insight. Finally, at the crown chakra, visualize violet or white and focus on spiritual connection and unity with the divine.

As you move through this meditation, allow yourself to feel the energy of each chakra being purified and activated by the Violet Flame. You may repeat the corresponding decrees for each chakra as you go, reinforcing the energy work with the power of the spoken word. This meditation can be done as a standalone practice or as part of your daily spiritual routine to maintain balance and alignment in your energy field.

Another powerful practice for balancing the chakras with the Violet Flame is color visualization. Since each chakra is associated with a specific color, working with these colors in combination with the Violet Flame can help to enhance the energy flow and bring greater harmony to your energy centers. This practice involves visualizing the Violet Flame surrounding each chakra while simultaneously focusing on the color that corresponds to that energy center.

Begin by visualizing the Violet Flame descending through your crown chakra, as you did in previous exercises. This time, however, as the flame moves through each chakra, see the flame merging with the color associated with that chakra. For example, at the root chakra, see the Violet Flame blending with red, creating a vibrant, glowing energy of both colors. At the sacral chakra, see the Violet Flame merging with orange, and so on.

As you work with the color visualization, focus on the qualities of each chakra and how the Violet Flame is enhancing them. At the root chakra, feel the grounding and stability that the red energy provides, and how the Violet Flame amplifies that feeling by transmuting any fears or insecurities. At the heart chakra, feel the love and compassion of the green or pink energy, and how the Violet Flame deepens your capacity for unconditional love by dissolving emotional pain or grief.

This color visualization technique helps to bring the chakras into greater alignment by combining the purifying energy of the Violet Flame with the vibrational frequency of each chakra's color. By working with both the flame and the color, you create a more powerful synergy that enhances the healing process and supports long-term balance.

As you continue to work with these techniques, you will develop a stronger connection to your chakras and a deeper understanding of how they influence your overall well-being. Regular practice will help you maintain energetic balance, prevent blockages, and ensure that your chakras are functioning in harmony with one another. This balance is essential not only for physical health but also for emotional stability, mental clarity, and spiritual growth.

Beyond personal chakra work, these techniques can also be used to help others. Whether you are working with clients or loved ones, you can guide them through similar practices to help them align and balance their energy centers. You may also use the Violet Flame in combination with color visualization or breathwork to support chakra healing for others, creating a powerful flow of energy that brings balance to their entire system.

The more you work with the chakras in this way, the more you will begin to notice shifts in your own energy and the energy of those around you. Balanced chakras lead to greater peace, clarity, and alignment with your higher self, allowing you to move through life with a sense of purpose and spiritual connection. These practices, combined with the transformative energy of the Violet Flame, offer a powerful path to holistic healing and spiritual awakening.

Chapter 14
Purifying Spaces with the Violet Flame

Our external environment can have a profound impact on our internal state of being. Just as we cleanse and protect our own energy field, it's equally important to purify the spaces in which we live and work. Energetic imprints, negative emotions, and lingering vibrations from past events can accumulate in physical spaces, affecting our well-being and the flow of energy. By working with the Violet Flame to cleanse these spaces, you can create a high-vibrational environment that supports your spiritual growth, healing, and overall well-being.

Every space carries an energetic signature, which is influenced by the thoughts, emotions, and actions of the people who inhabit or visit it. Over time, spaces can become cluttered with energetic debris, especially if there has been conflict, stress, illness, or other lower vibrational experiences. These energies can linger in the environment, creating a sense of heaviness, discomfort, or stagnation. Regularly purifying your space with the Violet Flame helps to clear away these negative influences, restoring harmony and balance to the environment.

To begin purifying a space, first choose a location that you would like to cleanse. This could be your home, office, meditation space, or any other area where you spend a significant amount of time. Before starting the purification process, take a few moments to center yourself and connect with the energy of the Violet Flame. Visualize a column of Violet Flame descending from above, surrounding your entire body and filling you with its purifying energy.

Once you feel connected to the Violet Flame, begin by walking through the space, holding the intention of cleansing and purifying the energy. As you move through each room, visualize the Violet Flame filling the space, dissolving any negative or stagnant energies. You can enhance this visualization by repeating a decree, such as: "I AM the Violet Flame, purifying this space and transmuting all lower energies into light." As you repeat the decree, feel the energy in the room becoming lighter and more harmonious.

As you continue walking through the space, focus on any areas that feel particularly heavy, stagnant, or uncomfortable. These areas might be corners of rooms, places where people frequently gather, or spots where emotional exchanges have occurred. In these areas, visualize the Violet Flame becoming more concentrated, burning away any lingering energies. See the flame transmuting negative emotions, thought forms, and any other discordant vibrations, transforming them into pure light.

You can also use visualization techniques to enhance the clearing process. Imagine that the Violet Flame is flowing through every part of the space, filling the walls, floors, and ceiling with its transformative energy. See the flame moving through every object in the room, purifying them and removing any unwanted energetic imprints. You may also visualize the Violet Flame moving through the air, clearing any residual thoughts or emotions that may be lingering in the atmosphere.

As you do this, it can be helpful to incorporate sacred geometry or specific patterns to guide the Violet Flame's energy. For example, imagine a grid of Violet Flame expanding throughout the room, connecting every corner and surface. This geometric visualization can help ensure that the entire space is being cleansed, leaving no part untouched by the flame's purifying light.

Another effective method for purifying spaces with the Violet Flame is through the use of sound. Sound waves have the ability to move through space, breaking up stagnant energy and allowing the Violet Flame to penetrate more deeply into the environment. You can use instruments such as a bell, chime, or singing bowl to create vibrations that enhance the energy clearing. As you move through the space, ring the bell or play the singing bowl, allowing the sound to carry the energy of the Violet Flame through the room. Visualize the sound waves dispersing any negative energy and creating a high-vibrational field in their wake.

As you work with sound, continue to repeat a cleansing decree, such as: "I AM the Violet Flame, purifying this space with sound and light, restoring perfect harmony and balance." This combination of sound and intention amplifies the Violet Flame's energy, making the clearing process more effective.

Crystals are another powerful tool for purifying spaces with the Violet Flame. Amethyst and clear quartz, in particular, are excellent for maintaining a high vibration and supporting the Violet Flame's cleansing properties. To use crystals in your space-clearing work, place an amethyst or clear quartz crystal in the center of each room you wish to cleanse. Visualize the Violet Flame flowing through the crystal, amplifying its energy and radiating it throughout the space.

As you place the crystal, repeat the decree: "I AM the Violet Flame, working through this crystal to cleanse and purify this space, filling it with divine light." The crystal acts as a conductor for the Violet Flame, enhancing its ability to transmute negative energy and maintain a high-vibrational environment. You may leave the crystals in place after the clearing to help sustain the positive energy of the space over time.

In some cases, you may wish to use herbs or essential oils to complement the Violet Flame in your space-clearing work. Sage, palo santo, and lavender are well-known for their ability to clear negative energy and raise the vibration of a space. To incorporate these tools, light a bundle of sage or palo santo and allow the smoke to move through the room, visualizing the Violet Flame following the path of the smoke. As the smoke rises, see it carrying away any negative energy, leaving the space purified and uplifted.

You may also create a cleansing spray using essential oils such as lavender or frankincense, diluted in water. Spray the mixture throughout the space, visualizing the Violet Flame moving through the air and purifying every corner. As you work with these natural elements, continue to repeat a decree such as: "I AM the Violet Flame, purifying this space with the elements of earth and spirit, restoring perfect peace and balance."

After you have completed the clearing process, it's important to seal the space with protective energy. This helps to prevent any unwanted energies from returning and ensures that the positive vibration is maintained. Visualize the Violet Flame surrounding the entire room, creating a protective barrier of light that shields the space from negative influences. You may repeat a decree such as: "I AM the Violet Flame, sealing this space with divine protection, ensuring that only love, light, and harmony may enter."

In addition to sealing the space with the Violet Flame, you can also invoke Archangel Michael and the Blue Flame of Protection. Visualize a bright blue light surrounding the room, reinforcing the protective barrier. Call upon Archangel Michael for assistance, saying: "Archangel Michael, please protect this space with your blue flame, ensuring that it remains clear, safe, and aligned with divine light." This added layer of protection ensures that the space remains energetically secure and free from discordant vibrations.

Regularly purifying and protecting your space with the Violet Flame is essential for maintaining a high-vibrational environment, especially if you are using the space for healing, meditation, or spiritual practice. Over time, you will notice a significant difference in the energy of your surroundings, as the space becomes more aligned with peace, clarity, and spiritual harmony. You will feel more centered, grounded, and supported in your spiritual work when your environment is energetically clear.

In addition to using the Violet Flame to purify your personal spaces, this practice can be extended to larger areas such as workplaces, public spaces, and even outdoor environments. By applying the same techniques, you can help raise the vibration of any space, creating a more harmonious and supportive energy for everyone who enters it. Whether you are working in your home, office, or even a community gathering space, the Violet Flame can be used to create an environment that nurtures healing, growth, and transformation.

Building on the methods of space purification introduced earlier, this chapter focuses on the practical techniques for space clearing using rituals and crystal arrangements to maximize the healing potential of the Violet Flame. These practices can be adapted to suit different spaces and needs, from daily maintenance of your home's energy to preparing a sacred space for healing sessions or meditation.

One of the most powerful techniques for space clearing is the use of a Violet Flame altar or grid. Creating an altar or grid that is specifically dedicated to the Violet Flame allows you to focus its energy in a concentrated way, helping to amplify the cleansing process and maintain a high-vibrational field over time.

To create a Violet Flame altar, start by choosing a central location in the room, such as a small table or shelf, where you can place sacred objects that represent the energy of the Violet Flame. You might include items such as an amethyst crystal, a violet candle, and a photo or statue of Saint Germain. Each of these objects serves as an anchor for the energy of the Violet Flame, helping to focus and direct its purifying power.

Once you have arranged your altar, take a few moments to connect with the energy of the Violet Flame. Visualize the flame surrounding the altar and all the objects on it, filling the space with its purifying light. You may wish to light the violet candle as a symbol of your intention to clear and protect the space. As the candle burns, repeat a decree such as: "I AM the Violet Flame, filling this altar and this space with divine light and protection." Allow the candle to burn for several minutes, or leave it burning throughout the day if possible, as a continual source of cleansing and transmutation.

For an even more powerful effect, consider creating a crystal grid around the altar using amethyst or clear quartz. Arrange the crystals in a geometric pattern, such as a circle or star, around the altar. Visualize the Violet Flame flowing through each crystal, amplifying its energy and radiating it throughout the space. You may repeat a decree such as: "I AM the Violet Flame, radiating through these crystals to cleanse and protect this space."

This altar or grid can be maintained as a permanent feature of your home or workspace, continually cleansing and protecting the space.

As the Violet Flame altar or grid continues to work, you'll notice that the energy of the space remains consistently higher in vibration, creating a sense of peace and harmony. This can be especially beneficial in spaces where healing work, meditation, or spiritual practices take place, as it helps maintain the purity and clarity of the environment. You may also find that the space feels lighter, more welcoming, and conducive to deeper spiritual connection.

In addition to maintaining an altar or grid, regular space-clearing rituals are highly effective for keeping the energy of a room or building clear and aligned. One such ritual involves combining the Violet Flame with intention setting and movement to cleanse and energize a space. To perform this ritual, begin by standing in the center of the room you wish to purify. Close your eyes and take a few deep breaths, grounding yourself and connecting with the energy of the Violet Flame. Visualize the flame surrounding your entire body, filling you with its purifying light.

Next, raise your arms and slowly begin to turn in a clockwise direction. As you turn, visualize the Violet Flame expanding outward from your body, filling the entire room with its energy. As the flame expands, see it dissolving any stagnant or negative energy, transforming the space into a field of pure light. As you continue turning, repeat a decree, such as: "I AM the Violet Flame, transmuting all lower energies in this space and restoring divine harmony." Continue this process until you have made a complete circle and feel that the room is fully cleansed.

If you prefer a more structured approach, you can also create a Violet Flame purification ceremony for larger spaces or special occasions. This type of ritual can be particularly useful for clearing the energy after significant events, such as gatherings, conflicts, or times of stress, where the energy may have become more heavily impacted. For this ceremony, gather tools such as candles, crystals, sage or palo santo, and a small bowl of water to represent the elements of fire, earth, air, and water.

Begin the ceremony by lighting the candle and sage or palo santo, invoking the presence of the Violet Flame and setting the intention for the purification. As you move through the space, visualize the flame surrounding each corner, wall, and object, clearing away any discordant energies. You may also sprinkle a few drops of water in each room to symbolize the cleansing power of water, further enhancing the purification process. At the end of the ceremony, place a crystal, such as amethyst, in the center of the room to anchor the purified energy and maintain the higher vibration.

Regular space clearing with the Violet Flame helps to keep the energy of your home, office, or sacred space aligned with the highest vibrations, ensuring that the environment supports your spiritual work and personal well-being. Whether through daily cleansing, creating a permanent altar or grid, or performing a full purification ceremony, these practices empower you to take control of the energy in your surroundings. By keeping your space energetically clear, you not only improve your environment but also enhance your ability to connect with divine energies, receive guidance, and support your own healing journey.

Ultimately, the power of the Violet Flame to transmute and purify extends far beyond the individual, offering a profound way to create and maintain sacred spaces that nurture healing, peace, and spiritual growth. By integrating these techniques into your daily life, you build a foundation of energetic protection and harmony, allowing both you and those around you to thrive in a purified and balanced environment.

Chapter 15
Healing Relationships with the Violet Flame

Relationships are at the core of human experience, shaping our emotional, mental, and spiritual lives. Whether they are personal, familial, or professional, relationships influence how we perceive the world and ourselves. At times, relationships can become challenging, strained by misunderstandings, emotional wounds, or unresolved conflicts. The Violet Flame offers a powerful way to heal relationships by transmuting the negative energies that create discord and replacing them with love, understanding, and harmony. By working with the Violet Flame, you can dissolve the emotional and energetic blockages that hinder healthy relationships and restore balance in your connections with others.

At the heart of relationship healing is the principle of forgiveness. Whether the conflict stems from a misunderstanding, a deep emotional wound, or long-standing tension, forgiveness is essential for releasing the past and moving forward with love and compassion. The Violet Flame is particularly effective in helping you release feelings of anger, resentment, guilt, or judgment—emotions that often block forgiveness and keep us trapped in negative cycles with others. By invoking the Violet Flame in relationship healing, you allow its transformative energy to dissolve the emotional barriers that prevent true forgiveness and reconciliation.

To begin using the Violet Flame to heal a relationship, it's important to first reflect on the specific relationship that needs healing. Take a few moments to sit quietly and focus on the person or people with whom you wish to heal your connection. Visualize their presence before you, and bring to mind the aspects of the relationship that feel strained or imbalanced. These might include feelings of hurt, betrayal, or unresolved anger, as well as any negative patterns that have developed between you.

Once you have a clear sense of the dynamics that need healing, call upon the energy of the Violet Flame. Visualize a column of Violet Flame descending from above, surrounding both you and the person with whom you are working. See the flame gently dissolving any negative or discordant energy that exists between you, including unspoken resentments, judgments, or emotional pain. As the Violet Flame works, imagine it transmuting these lower vibrations into pure light, restoring peace and balance between you.

As you visualize the Violet Flame working between you, it can be helpful to repeat a forgiveness decree, such as: "I AM the Violet Flame, transmuting all pain, anger, and discord in this relationship and restoring perfect love and harmony." With each repetition of the decree, feel the energy between you becoming lighter, as the flame continues to dissolve the emotional barriers and blockages that have contributed to the conflict.

In addition to working with the Violet Flame for forgiveness, another key element in relationship healing is compassion. Compassion allows you to see beyond the surface of conflict and misunderstandings, recognizing the deeper emotional needs and experiences of the other person. When you approach a relationship from a place of compassion, you open the door to healing and understanding, even in situations where communication has broken down or emotions have run high.

To cultivate compassion in your relationships, begin by placing your hands over your heart and visualizing the Violet Flame filling your heart center with its purifying energy. As the flame burns brightly in your heart, see it expanding outward, filling your entire body with love and compassion. As you focus on this energy, bring to mind the person with whom you are seeking healing. Rather than focusing on the conflict, imagine seeing this person through the eyes of compassion, recognizing their struggles, pain, and needs.

As the Violet Flame works to expand your heart, you may repeat a compassion decree, such as: "I AM the Violet Flame, filling my heart with love and compassion, seeing this relationship through the eyes of divine understanding." As you repeat this decree, feel your heart softening and opening to a new perspective, one that allows you to embrace the other person with empathy and kindness, regardless of past misunderstandings or hurt.

When working with the Violet Flame to heal relationships, it's important to acknowledge that healing does not always mean restoring the relationship to its previous form. In some cases, healing may involve creating new boundaries, letting go of old patterns, or even releasing the relationship entirely. The Violet Flame helps you to approach these decisions with clarity and love, ensuring that whatever steps you take are aligned with your highest good and the highest good of all involved.

For example, if you find that a relationship is no longer serving your spiritual or emotional growth, the Violet Flame can assist you in releasing it with grace and compassion. To do this, visualize the Violet Flame surrounding both you and the person from whom you are seeking to release. See the flame gently dissolving any attachments, cords, or emotional ties that no longer serve your highest purpose. As the Violet Flame works, repeat a release decree, such as: "I AM the Violet Flame, releasing all attachments to this relationship, restoring peace and freedom for both of us." This process allows you to release the relationship without anger or resentment, creating space for both parties to heal and grow in their own ways.

In cases where the relationship is deeply important to you and you wish to strengthen it, the Violet Flame can help to rebuild the bond by fostering greater communication, trust, and emotional intimacy. One technique for deepening a relationship is to use the Violet Flame to cleanse and energize the heart connection between you and the other person. Begin by focusing on your own heart chakra, visualizing the Violet Flame purifying and expanding this energy center. Once your heart chakra feels balanced, visualize a stream of Violet Flame energy flowing from your heart to the heart of the other person.

As the Violet Flame flows between your hearts, see it clearing away any misunderstandings, judgments, or emotional barriers that may have developed over time. Visualize the flame strengthening the bond between you, filling both of your hearts with love, understanding, and mutual respect. As you work with this visualization, repeat a decree such as: "I AM the Violet Flame, healing and strengthening the heart connection between us, restoring perfect love and trust." With each repetition of the decree, feel the energy between you becoming stronger and more harmonious.

In addition to using the Violet Flame for direct relationship healing, you can also work with this energy to heal family dynamics. Family relationships are often complex, carrying emotional patterns that may have been passed down through generations. These patterns can create tension, misunderstandings, or emotional distance, even when there is love and care between family members. The Violet Flame offers a way to heal these generational patterns, transmuting the negative energy that has accumulated over time and restoring harmony within the family unit.

To begin healing family dynamics with the Violet Flame, take some time to reflect on the specific patterns or relationships within your family that feel imbalanced. These might include unresolved conflicts, unspoken resentments, or patterns of behavior that create tension. Once you have identified the dynamics that need healing, call upon the Violet Flame to transmute the negative energy within the family. Visualize the flame surrounding your entire family, dissolving the emotional wounds and negative patterns that have been carried through generations.

You may repeat a decree such as: "I AM the Violet Flame, transmuting all discord and negative patterns within my family, restoring peace, love, and harmony to our relationships." As you work with this decree, imagine the Violet Flame purifying not only the current generation but also the ancestral patterns that have contributed to the challenges within your family. By working with the Violet Flame in this way, you help to release the emotional baggage that has been passed down, allowing for healing and growth in your family relationships.

The healing power of the Violet Flame extends far beyond the individual, offering a profound way to transform the dynamics of relationships at every level. Whether you are working to heal a personal connection, restore harmony within your family, or release a relationship that no longer serves you, the Violet Flame provides the energy of transmutation, forgiveness, and compassion. By integrating these practices into your life, you can experience deeper, more fulfilling relationships, free from the emotional baggage and negative patterns that often hinder love and connection.

As you continue working with the Violet Flame to heal relationships, you will find that the energy of love, understanding, and forgiveness becomes more accessible in all your interactions. This not only strengthens your personal and family relationships but also enhances your capacity to offer love and healing to the world around you.

One of the most powerful techniques for healing relationships is the Violet Flame invocation ritual. This ritual allows you to call upon the energy of the Violet Flame to transmute the negative emotions, patterns, and energetic blockages that are contributing to discord in a relationship. To begin, create a quiet and sacred space where you can focus your intention. Light a candle, preferably violet in color, and place a photo or a symbolic object representing the person with whom you seek healing on an altar or table.

Sit comfortably in front of the candle, close your eyes, and take a few deep breaths to center yourself. Visualize the Violet Flame surrounding you, filling your heart and aura with its purifying energy. As you breathe in, feel the Violet Flame expanding within you, dissolving any personal negative emotions or judgments you may be carrying in the relationship. This is an important step, as it helps clear your own energy before you begin working on the relationship itself.

Once you feel centered and clear, shift your focus to the relationship you are working to heal. Visualize the person in front of you, surrounded by the Violet Flame. As the flame envelops them, see it dissolving any negative energies, misunderstandings, or emotional wounds that may have developed between you. You may say aloud: "I invoke the Violet Flame to surround and heal this relationship, dissolving all discord, pain, and misunderstanding. I call upon the Flame to restore harmony, love, and peace between us."

As you hold this visualization, allow the Violet Flame to work between you and the other person, transmuting all the lower vibrations into light. This might include old arguments, emotional pain, or lingering resentments. As the flame works, you may notice feelings of lightness or relief as the emotional weight is lifted. You can enhance the energy of the ritual by repeating a decree such as: "I AM the Violet Flame, healing all divisions and restoring divine love and understanding in this relationship."

Another effective method for healing relationships with the Violet Flame is cord cutting. Emotional and energetic cords often form between people in relationships, especially when there has been conflict, tension, or prolonged emotional exchanges. These cords can drain energy, keep both parties stuck in negative patterns, and prevent true healing from taking place. Cord cutting with the Violet Flame allows you to release these attachments while maintaining the love and respect in the relationship.

To perform a cord-cutting ritual, begin by sitting in a quiet space and taking a few moments to ground and center yourself. Visualize the Violet Flame surrounding your entire body, purifying your energy and preparing you for the healing work ahead. Next, bring to mind the person with whom you share a cord. This could be someone with whom you have unresolved conflict or emotional ties that no longer serve your highest good.

As you visualize the person in front of you, imagine an energetic cord extending between your heart and theirs. This cord represents the emotional and energetic attachment that has formed over time. It may carry emotions such as fear, guilt, anger, or resentment—energies that weigh down the relationship and prevent healing. Call upon the Violet Flame to dissolve this cord. See the flame gently burning away the negative attachments between you, while preserving the love, compassion, and mutual respect that remain in the relationship.

As the cord dissolves, repeat a decree such as: "I AM the Violet Flame, cutting all negative attachments in this relationship, restoring freedom, love, and harmony for both of us." Feel the energy between you becoming lighter and more harmonious as the cord is transmuted into light. Once the cord is fully dissolved, visualize the Violet Flame surrounding both you and the other person, sealing your energy fields and protecting you from any future attachments that may form. This practice allows both parties to move forward with greater clarity and emotional freedom.

In cases where a relationship has become particularly strained, such as a family relationship or a long-term partnership, a more in-depth healing practice may be required. One powerful technique is the Violet Flame forgiveness meditation, which focuses on releasing deeply embedded emotional pain and resentment. This meditation helps to create space for reconciliation and emotional healing, even in situations where communication has broken down or where forgiveness seems difficult.

To practice the Violet Flame forgiveness meditation, find a comfortable and quiet place where you won't be disturbed. Begin by taking several deep breaths, allowing yourself to relax and release any tension. Visualize the Violet Flame surrounding your heart center, filling it with its transformative energy. As the flame burns brightly in your heart, see it dissolving any anger, pain, or resentment that you may be holding toward the person in question. Feel these emotions being transmuted into love, compassion, and forgiveness.

Next, visualize the other person's heart also being surrounded by the Violet Flame. As the flame works, imagine it dissolving any negative emotions they may be carrying toward you, whether they are conscious of them or not. See the Violet Flame bridging the space between your hearts, creating a flow of healing energy that restores peace and understanding between you. As you hold this visualization, repeat a decree such as: "I AM the Violet Flame, forgiving and healing this relationship, dissolving all discord and restoring divine love and peace."

This meditation can be repeated as often as needed to support the healing process. It is particularly effective when used regularly, as it helps to break down the emotional walls that have been built up over time, allowing both parties to experience a deeper sense of forgiveness and reconciliation.

Another powerful tool for relationship healing is working with the Violet Flame through written decrees or affirmations. Writing down your intentions and repeating them regularly helps to anchor the energy of the Violet Flame into the relationship, reinforcing the healing process over time. You can create your own decrees based on the specific dynamics of the relationship, or you can use one of the following examples:

"I AM the Violet Flame, transmuting all negativity in my relationship with [name], restoring perfect love, understanding, and harmony."

"I call upon the Violet Flame to heal all pain, anger, and discord between me and [name]. I release all judgment and embrace forgiveness."

"With the power of the Violet Flame, I dissolve all emotional blockages and restore balance, peace, and compassion in my relationship with [name]."

Writing these decrees down in a journal and repeating them aloud each day amplifies their effect, allowing the Violet Flame to work continuously to heal and restore the relationship.

Finally, for long-term healing, it's important to create an ongoing practice of maintaining the positive energy in your relationships through the Violet Flame. This can be done through regular visualization, meditation, or even small daily rituals where you invoke the Violet Flame to support harmony in your relationships. For example, each morning you might take a few moments to visualize the Violet Flame surrounding you and the important people in your life, offering protection, healing, and balance. You might repeat a simple decree, such as: "I AM the Violet Flame, blessing all my relationships with love, peace, and understanding."

By incorporating these practices into your daily life, you create a strong energetic foundation that supports the ongoing health and harmony of your relationships. The Violet Flame becomes a constant presence, working behind the scenes to dissolve any negativity that may arise, while amplifying the love and compassion that form the basis of healthy connections.

As you continue to work with the Violet Flame for relationship healing, you will notice a profound transformation not only in your interactions with others but also in how you view relationships as a whole. The energy of the Violet Flame helps you to release old patterns, embrace forgiveness, and cultivate deeper levels of empathy, understanding, and love. These qualities, when nurtured, lead to more fulfilling and harmonious relationships, where both parties are free to grow and thrive together.

Chapter 16
Working with Spiritual Guides in Healing

In the process of holistic healing, one of the most powerful resources available to us is the assistance of spiritual guides, angels, and beings of light. These higher-dimensional entities offer wisdom, guidance, and protection as we navigate the complexities of healing ourselves and others. Saint Germain himself, often seen as a master of spiritual wisdom, works closely with other ascended beings to guide healers in accessing higher realms of consciousness. By learning how to communicate with these spiritual guides, we open the door to deeper healing, greater insight, and profound spiritual growth.

Every person has spiritual guides that accompany them throughout life. These guides may include angels, ancestors, ascended masters like Saint Germain, or other enlightened beings who offer assistance when called upon. While some individuals may feel a natural connection to these guides, others may not yet be aware of their presence. Regardless of our level of awareness, spiritual guides are always available to help us, especially when we are engaged in healing work. Their presence can enhance the effectiveness of healing sessions, offering support, clarity, and protection for both the healer and the recipient of the healing energy.

The first step in working with spiritual guides is developing a conscious awareness of their presence. This often begins with the practice of quieting the mind through meditation and setting the intention to connect with your guides. Find a calm and peaceful place where you can meditate without distractions. Close your eyes, take a few deep breaths, and allow yourself to relax fully. Visualize a soft, white light surrounding you, offering protection and peace. As you focus on your breath, silently invite your spiritual guides to make their presence known.

You may say a simple invocation such as: "I call upon my spiritual guides and angels to assist me in this healing process. I invite your guidance, protection, and wisdom as I work to align with the highest good." As you repeat this intention, remain open to the subtle signs of their presence. You may sense a shift in energy, feel a loving warmth, or receive an intuitive message or image in your mind's eye. Trust that your guides are with you, even if you do not immediately sense them in a tangible way.

Once you have established a connection with your spiritual guides, you can begin to ask for their assistance in healing. Your guides offer help in many ways, from providing insight into the root causes of physical or emotional issues to offering protection and support as you channel healing energy. During a healing session, you may silently ask your guides for clarity, particularly if you feel unsure about how to approach a specific issue. You may ask questions such as: "What does this person need most right now to support their healing?" or "How can I best assist in releasing this block?"

One of the most profound ways spiritual guides can assist in healing is by helping to reveal energetic blockages or imbalances that may not be immediately apparent. These blockages often manifest in the form of emotional pain, trauma, or karmic patterns that are stored in the energy body. By asking your guides for help in identifying these areas of imbalance, you gain access to insights that might otherwise remain hidden. For example, you may sense a particular area of the body where the energy feels heavy or stagnant, or you may receive an intuitive image or feeling that points to a past emotional wound that needs to be addressed.

When this type of insight arises, it is essential to remain open to the guidance being offered. Allow yourself to trust the impressions you receive, even if they come in subtle or unexpected forms. As you work with the Violet Flame to transmute the negative energy, ask your guides to assist in clearing the blockages and restoring balance to the person's energy field. You may say something like: "I ask for your assistance in clearing this block with the energy of the Violet Flame, dissolving all negativity and restoring divine harmony."

In addition to helping you identify and clear blockages, your spiritual guides can also offer protection during healing work. Healing sessions often involve the movement and release of heavy or dense energy, and without proper protection, the healer may inadvertently absorb some of this energy. By calling upon your guides for protection, you create an energetic shield around yourself and the person you are working with, ensuring that both of you remain safe and energetically clear.

To invoke protection, you can call upon Archangel Michael, a powerful protector who works closely with Saint Germain and the Violet Flame. Visualize a brilliant blue light surrounding your body and the space where the healing is taking place. This blue light, the energy of the Blue Flame of Protection, creates a powerful barrier that shields you from any negative or discordant energies. You may say a protection decree such as: "I call upon Archangel Michael and the Blue Flame to protect me and this space from all negative energies. Let only love and divine light enter here."

Spiritual guides not only assist in physical healing but also offer profound emotional and spiritual healing. When working with someone who is struggling with grief, trauma, or feelings of disconnection, your guides can offer guidance on how to provide emotional support. They may direct you to focus on specific areas of the energy body or guide you to use particular healing techniques, such as the Violet Flame, to transmute the emotional pain.

During emotional healing sessions, it can be helpful to ask your guides to offer the recipient a sense of comfort and peace. You may say a simple invocation such as: "I ask that my spiritual guides and angels surround [the person's name] with love, comfort, and healing. Help them to release any pain, grief, or fear, and fill their heart with divine peace." As you hold this intention, visualize the person being surrounded by loving light, knowing that your guides are offering their support throughout the healing process.

Over time, as you deepen your connection with your spiritual guides, you may find that they offer messages of encouragement, wisdom, or insight for the person you are healing. These messages can come in the form of intuitive impressions, visions, or even direct communication from the guides themselves. If you receive such a message during a healing session, trust that it is being offered for the highest good of the person involved. You may choose to share the message with them, if appropriate, or simply allow the energy of the message to be integrated into the healing work.

Finally, remember that working with spiritual guides is a collaborative process. While your guides offer wisdom, insight, and support, they also respect your free will and the choices of the person receiving healing. Their role is not to take control but to work alongside you, helping to facilitate the healing process in a way that honors each person's unique path. By maintaining an open heart and a willingness to receive their guidance, you create a powerful partnership that enhances your ability to offer holistic and transformative healing.

As you continue to cultivate your relationship with your spiritual guides, you will find that their presence becomes an integral part of your healing work. Whether you are healing yourself, others, or the planet, their assistance allows you to access higher realms of wisdom and spiritual power, helping to elevate the vibration of the healing process and bring about profound and lasting transformation.

Having established a connection with spiritual guides and begun to work with their energy in healing. The key to effectively working with spiritual guides during healing sessions is learning to trust your intuitive connection, refining your communication methods, and developing rituals or processes that invite their presence in a clear and intentional way. With these tools, you can amplify the healing potential of your sessions, both for yourself and those you assist.

One powerful method for strengthening your connection with spiritual guides is the practice of automatic writing or intuitive journaling. This technique allows you to receive direct messages from your guides in written form, offering clarity and insight that can support your healing work. To begin, find a quiet space where you can sit with a journal and pen. Take a few moments to center yourself through deep breathing or meditation, and then set the intention to receive guidance from your spiritual guides.

As you sit in a receptive state, invite your guides to communicate with you through writing. You may ask a specific question related to a healing issue or simply open yourself to whatever message they wish to share. Begin writing whatever thoughts, impressions, or images come to mind, without judgment or overthinking. Allow the words to flow naturally, trusting that your guides are communicating through your intuition. This practice can offer profound insights into the root causes of physical or emotional imbalances, as well as guidance on how to approach the healing process.

For example, if you are working with a client who is experiencing chronic illness, you might use automatic writing to ask your guides for insights into the energetic root of the condition. You may receive messages related to emotional blockages, past traumas, or karmic patterns that are contributing to the illness. These insights can then be integrated into your healing sessions, helping to address the underlying issues and facilitate deeper healing.

Another effective technique for working with spiritual guides is the use of guided meditations that specifically focus on invoking their presence and receiving healing support. These meditations help to create a direct line of communication with your guides, allowing you to ask for their assistance in real-time during healing work. You can create your own guided meditation or use pre-recorded ones that are designed to facilitate connection with spiritual beings.

To create your own meditation, begin by visualizing a sacred space—a place where you feel safe, peaceful, and open to receiving divine guidance. This space might be a garden, a temple, or a beautiful landscape. Imagine yourself sitting in this space, surrounded by light and tranquility. Once you feel fully immersed in this environment, call upon your spiritual guides to join you. Visualize their presence in whatever form feels most natural to you—perhaps as beings of light, angels, or ascended masters.

As your guides join you in this sacred space, you can begin to communicate with them. Ask for their support in healing a specific issue, either for yourself or someone you are working with. You may say something like: "I ask for your assistance in healing [name]'s energy. Please guide me to understand what is needed for their highest good." As you pose this question, remain open to any impressions, feelings, or images that arise. Your guides may offer you insights through symbols, intuitive messages, or even direct verbal communication. Trust that whatever comes through is intended to support the healing process.

Once you have received guidance from your spiritual guides, you can integrate their wisdom into your healing work. For instance, they may suggest that you focus on a particular energy center, such as the heart chakra, or guide you to use a specific healing technique, such as the Violet Flame, to transmute emotional pain. As you follow their guidance, you will notice that your healing sessions become more fluid, intuitive, and effective.

In addition to using meditation and journaling, it's helpful to create rituals or ceremonies that invite the presence of your spiritual guides at the start of each healing session. This helps to establish a clear intention and create a sacred space where healing energy can flow freely. A simple yet powerful ritual involves lighting a candle or burning incense before the session begins. As you do so, set the intention to invite your guides into the space, asking them to offer protection, insight, and support throughout the healing process.

You may say a prayer or invocation such as: "I call upon my spiritual guides and angels to join me in this healing session. Please guide me with your wisdom, protect the space with your light, and help me to channel the highest healing energy for [name]." As you make this invocation, visualize the space being filled with light and the presence of your guides. Feel their energy surrounding you, offering support and protection as you prepare to begin the healing work.

Throughout the session, maintain an open dialogue with your guides. You can ask for their guidance at any point, especially if you encounter a challenge or feel unsure about how to proceed. For example, if you are working with someone who is experiencing a deep emotional block, you might ask your guides: "What is the source of this block, and how can I help release it?" Remain open to their response, whether it comes in the form of a feeling, a visual image, or a direct message. Your guides may direct you to focus on a specific chakra, use a particular healing tool, or offer a message of comfort and reassurance to the person you are working with.

Spiritual guides are not only valuable for providing insight and support during healing sessions; they also play a crucial role in offering protection. Healing work often involves the release of heavy or negative energies, which can sometimes cling to the healer or the environment if not properly cleared. By calling upon your spiritual guides, particularly protective beings such as Archangel Michael, you ensure that both you and the healing space remain energetically safe.

Before beginning a session, visualize the healing space being surrounded by a protective light, either violet or blue, representing the Violet Flame and the protective energy of Archangel Michael. Ask your guides to seal the space, preventing any lower energies from entering or affecting the healing process. You may say a protection decree such as: "I call upon the Violet

Flame and Archangel Michael to protect this space and all those within it. Let only love, light, and healing energy enter here."

In addition to shielding the space, your guides can also help you clear any energy that may be lingering after a session. After completing the healing work, take a few moments to thank your spiritual guides for their assistance. Visualize the Violet Flame sweeping through the room, dissolving any residual energy and restoring the space to its natural state of purity and light. You can also ask your guides to help you clear your own energy, especially if you feel fatigued or heavy after the session. Simply visualize the Violet Flame surrounding your body, transmuting any negative or stagnant energy and replacing it with fresh, vibrant light.

Over time, as you continue to develop your relationship with your spiritual guides, you will find that they become trusted allies in your healing work. Their presence adds a layer of spiritual depth and protection, allowing you to access higher realms of consciousness and healing power. Whether you are working on yourself or others, the guidance and support of spiritual beings offer profound insight and clarity, helping to facilitate deeper healing on all levels—physical, emotional, mental, and spiritual.

As you cultivate this connection, remember that your guides are always available to assist you, both during formal healing sessions and in your everyday life. By maintaining a regular practice of connecting with them through meditation, prayer, or ritual, you strengthen your intuitive abilities and enhance your capacity to offer holistic and transformative healing to yourself and others.

Chapter 17
Holistic Healing in Children -

Children, with their vibrant energy and open spirits, respond uniquely to holistic healing practices. Their energy fields are often more sensitive and malleable than those of adults, which means that healing techniques can have a profound and immediate impact on their physical, emotional, and spiritual well-being. However, because of this heightened sensitivity, it is essential to approach healing in children with gentleness and care, ensuring that the methods used are adapted to their developmental stage and energetic needs.

Holistic healing in children involves recognizing that their physical ailments or emotional struggles are often linked to imbalances in their energy bodies. Like adults, children have energy centers (or chakras) that influence their overall health, though these centers may still be developing and are often more susceptible to external influences. Moreover, children are deeply connected to their environment and can easily absorb the emotions and energies of those around them—whether from family members, peers, or even the spaces they inhabit. For this reason, it's important to create a supportive and nurturing environment that fosters their healing.

One of the first steps in healing children holistically is working with the energy of the auric field. The auric field surrounds the body and acts as a protective layer, filtering energies that enter and leave the child's energetic space. When a child's auric field becomes weakened or damaged—due to illness, emotional stress, or exposure to negative environments—they may experience physical symptoms such as fatigue, frequent illness, or emotional difficulties like anxiety or irritability.

Strengthening and cleansing the auric field helps restore the child's energetic balance and promotes overall well-being.

A gentle way to cleanse a child's auric field is by using visualization techniques combined with the Violet Flame. To begin, sit with the child in a calm and peaceful environment. Depending on the child's age, you can invite them to sit quietly with their eyes closed, or simply hold them close while you perform the energy work. Visualize the Violet Flame descending from above and gently surrounding the child's body, enveloping them in a protective cocoon of light. See the flame moving through their aura, dissolving any negative or stagnant energy that may have accumulated.

As you hold this visualization, you may say aloud or silently: "I call upon the Violet Flame to cleanse and protect [child's name], dissolving all negative energies and restoring perfect balance and peace." This simple practice not only helps cleanse the child's energy field but also provides a sense of safety and comfort, allowing them to feel energetically protected. You can perform this visualization daily or whenever the child seems emotionally or physically out of balance.

In addition to working with the auric field, holistic healing for children also involves balancing their chakras. Just as adults have seven main chakras, children's chakras play a crucial role in their physical, emotional, and spiritual health. However, because children are still growing and developing, their chakras may not yet be fully formed or activated. This means that chakra work with children must be approached gently, with a focus on fostering healthy development rather than forcing rapid changes.

One of the simplest ways to balance a child's chakras is through color visualization and breathing exercises. Each chakra is associated with a specific color, and by visualizing these colors, you can help bring the child's energy centers into alignment. Begin by sitting with the child and encouraging them to take a few deep breaths. You can explain to them that you will be helping their body feel strong and balanced by using the power of colors.

Start with the root chakra, located at the base of the spine, which governs feelings of safety and security. Ask the child to imagine the color red at the base of their spine, glowing like a warm, steady light. As they breathe in, have them imagine that this red light is growing stronger, filling their body with a sense of safety and grounding. You can say something like: "As you breathe in, imagine this red light getting brighter, helping you feel safe and strong."

Next, move to the sacral chakra, located just below the navel, associated with creativity and emotions. Invite the child to visualize an orange light in this area, growing brighter with each breath. As they breathe, encourage them to imagine this light helping them feel happy, creative, and confident in expressing their emotions. Repeat this process for each chakra, using the corresponding colors: yellow for the solar plexus (personal power), green or pink for the heart chakra (love and compassion), blue for the throat chakra (communication), indigo for the third eye (intuition), and violet or white for the crown chakra (spiritual connection).

This color visualization practice can be adapted based on the child's age and level of understanding. For younger children, you might keep the explanations simple, focusing on how the colors help them feel strong, happy, or calm. Older children may enjoy learning more about the meaning of each chakra and how balancing these energy centers helps them feel better emotionally and physically.

Another important aspect of holistic healing for children is emotional support. Children often express their emotional needs through physical symptoms, such as headaches, stomachaches, or unexplained fatigue. These symptoms may indicate underlying emotional issues such as anxiety, fear, or sadness that the child may not yet have the words to articulate. In these cases, using the Violet Flame to transmute emotional energy can be incredibly effective.

To help a child release emotional tension, begin by creating a safe and comforting environment. Sit with the child and explain that they can let go of any worries or heavy feelings by imagining them being transformed into light. Ask the child to close their eyes and imagine the Violet Flame in their heart center, burning away any sadness, anger, or fear. As the flame burns, the heavy feelings are turned into light, leaving them feeling calm and happy.

As you guide the child through this visualization, you may repeat a soothing affirmation such as: "The Violet Flame is helping you let go of all your worries. You are safe, loved, and protected." This simple practice helps children understand that they have the power to release difficult emotions, empowering them to take an active role in their own emotional healing.

In cases where a child is dealing with deeper emotional wounds—such as trauma, grief, or bullying—additional support may be needed. In these situations, working with the heart chakra and encouraging the child to connect with their innate capacity for love and compassion can be particularly healing. Visualizations, meditations, or simply spending time with the child in a nurturing environment can help them feel supported as they process these emotions.

Another gentle method of emotional healing for children involves working with crystals. Crystals are often appealing to children because of their colors and tactile qualities, making them a natural tool for healing. Specific crystals, such as amethyst, rose quartz, and aventurine, can be particularly effective in promoting emotional balance and calming anxiety.

To use crystals with children, you can place a small crystal in their hand or near their body during meditation or bedtime. Encourage the child to hold the crystal and imagine that it is filling their body with light and peace. You might explain that the crystal is helping them feel calm, brave, or happy, depending on the emotional support they need at that moment. Children often form a natural connection to crystals, and they may find comfort in keeping one close to them, especially during times of stress.

Holistic healing for children also involves teaching them simple self-care practices that empower them to take care of their own energy. This can include teaching them basic breathing exercises, introducing them to affirmations, or helping them create a nighttime routine that includes calming rituals such as visualization or gentle music. By giving children tools to manage their own emotions and energy, you help them build a foundation of emotional intelligence and resilience that will serve them throughout their lives.

When working with children in any healing capacity, it's important to remember that play and creativity are vital components of their healing process. Children are naturally drawn to imaginative play, and incorporating elements of creativity into their healing can make the process both fun and effective. You might use stories, art, or games to help children explore their emotions and learn about their energy bodies. For example, you could invite a child to draw a picture of their energy field or create a story where they are a superhero using the Violet Flame to protect themselves and others.

By making healing a playful and engaging experience, children are more likely to embrace the process and feel empowered by their own ability to heal. Holistic healing for children is not just about addressing physical or emotional symptoms—it's about nurturing their spirit, honoring their unique energy, and helping them develop the tools they need to thrive in a balanced and harmonious way.

As we delve deeper into the practical applications of holistic healing for children, it becomes essential to understand the importance of gentle techniques that respect their delicate energy systems. Children are often more intuitive and energetically open than adults, which means they can quickly absorb both positive and negative energies from their surroundings. Healing methods for children should therefore emphasize protection, balance, and nurturing.

One of the most effective ways to support a child's holistic healing is through meditation and visualization techniques designed to suit their age and attention span. Meditation for children doesn't need to be long or complex. Simple, guided visualizations can help them feel centered and safe while encouraging emotional healing and energetic balance.

To introduce children to meditation, create a calming environment where they feel comfortable. Sit together, and explain that you'll be doing an activity to help them feel more peaceful and happy. Begin with a short guided meditation that focuses on relaxation and protection. You might ask the child to close their eyes and take a few deep breaths. Then, invite them to imagine themselves in a safe, beautiful place, like a garden or a magical forest.

In this imagined space, introduce the Violet Flame by asking the child to visualize a soft, glowing violet light surrounding their body, like a warm blanket of light. Explain that this light is helping to keep them safe and strong, dissolving any worries or fears they might have. You can say something like, "This special light is keeping you safe, and as it shines around you, it helps you feel calm and happy. Nothing bad can come through this light—it's here to protect you." This type of visualization not only introduces the child to the concept of energy protection but also helps them to build a relationship with the Violet Flame in a way that feels comforting and accessible.

Affirmations and decrees are another powerful tool for healing, and they can be tailored to children in simple, positive language. Decrees are statements spoken aloud that direct spiritual energy toward a specific intention. For children, using decrees can be both empowering and soothing, especially when they feel overwhelmed or uncertain. An easy decree for children to use might be: "I AM surrounded by love and light, and I feel safe and happy." This affirmation helps them connect with the energy of protection, love, and inner peace.

You can encourage children to repeat their affirmations or decrees daily, especially in moments when they are feeling anxious or sad. These simple phrases, when spoken regularly, help children shift their focus from fear or discomfort to feelings of safety, joy, and empowerment. By repeating decrees, children also learn that they have the ability to influence their own emotional and energetic state, which can be a powerful realization for young minds.

Another important aspect of holistic healing for children is teaching them to clear and protect their energy. As children are naturally open and sensitive, they can easily pick up energies from others, whether it's the stress of a family member, tension at school, or even residual energies from the spaces they inhabit. Teaching children how to clear and protect their energy is essential for their emotional and physical well-being.

One simple technique is to encourage children to imagine brushing off any unwanted energy at the end of the day, as though they were brushing dust off their clothes. You can explain that sometimes they might pick up feelings or thoughts that don't belong to them, and this practice helps them feel light and free again. Ask the child to run their hands over their body, from the top of their head down to their feet, as though brushing away any invisible energy that feels heavy or uncomfortable. While they do this, you might say, "We're brushing off all the things that don't belong to you—now you're clean and light!"

For older children, you can introduce the shielding technique, which involves visualizing a protective bubble of light surrounding their body. This bubble of light can be any color they choose, but violet is especially powerful because it carries the transmutational energy of the Violet Flame. As they imagine this bubble of light, explain that it acts as a shield, keeping them safe from any negative or unwanted energy. They can picture the light growing stronger and brighter every time they breathe in, and with each exhale, they can imagine any negativity being pushed out of their space.

You might guide them through a decree such as: "I AM the Violet Flame, protecting my space and filling it with love and light." This practice not only empowers children to take control of their energetic environment but also helps them develop a sense of emotional autonomy, knowing that they can create a safe space around themselves whenever they need it.

For children dealing with more intense emotions or trauma, using the Violet Flame in combination with crystals can be especially effective. Crystals have natural healing properties and are often very appealing to children due to their colors, textures, and shapes. Specific crystals, such as amethyst and rose quartz, are particularly helpful in calming emotions and promoting feelings of love and security.

To incorporate crystals into a child's healing practice, select a small crystal that resonates with the child. For example, rose quartz is often used to promote self-love and emotional healing, while amethyst is calming and protective. You can guide the child to hold the crystal in their hands while you lead them through a short Violet Flame meditation. Ask them to close their eyes and visualize the crystal glowing with violet light, surrounding them with peace and love. Explain that the crystal, combined with the Violet Flame, is helping to dissolve any worries or sadness and is filling them with happiness.

Encourage the child to keep the crystal in a special place, such as under their pillow, in their pocket, or on their bedside table. Knowing that they have this crystal nearby can offer them comfort, especially during times of emotional stress. Additionally, you can teach children how to "charge" their crystals with positive intentions by holding the crystal and repeating an affirmation, such as: "This crystal helps me feel happy and safe."

Another gentle but effective practice for children is the use of herbal baths. Bathing in water infused with calming herbs, such as lavender or chamomile, can have a soothing effect on both the physical and energetic body. To prepare a healing bath, steep a handful of dried herbs in hot water and pour the herbal infusion into the bath. As the child bathes, you can guide them through a visualization, asking them to imagine that the water is filled with the Violet Flame. Explain that as they soak in the water, the Violet Flame is gently washing away any feelings of sadness, fear, or discomfort, leaving them refreshed and full of light.

In some cases, particularly with younger children, it's important to use storytelling as a way of conveying healing concepts. Children relate deeply to stories, and you can create narratives that incorporate healing elements like the Violet Flame, crystals, or protective light. For example, you might tell a bedtime story about a child who, with the help of the Violet Flame, overcomes their fears and brings light and love to their family or community. These stories can serve as powerful metaphors for healing and help children internalize these concepts in a way that feels natural and engaging.

Lastly, it's important to remember that children often mirror the emotional and energetic states of their caregivers. Therefore, ensuring that the family environment is balanced and harmonious is crucial to the child's holistic healing. Encourage practices that the whole family can engage in, such as group meditations, creating a peaceful home atmosphere, or practicing daily affirmations together. When children see their family members participating in healing activities, they are more likely to feel supported and inspired to engage in their own healing journey.

Holistic healing for children is ultimately about empowerment—teaching them that they have the ability to influence their own well-being and providing them with tools that foster emotional intelligence, resilience, and energetic balance. The Violet Flame, combined with other gentle healing practices, offers children a safe, loving, and effective pathway to release negative energies and nurture their natural sense of joy, curiosity, and light. As they grow and evolve, these early practices become the foundation for a lifetime of holistic well-being, ensuring that they move forward with confidence, peace, and a strong connection to their own healing power.

Chapter 18
Preparing Crystal Elixirs and the Violet Flame

The healing power of crystals is well-known in holistic practices, and when combined with the transmutational energy of the Violet Flame, their effectiveness is amplified. Crystals possess unique energetic properties that resonate with specific frequencies, allowing them to aid in healing, protection, and spiritual growth. Preparing crystal elixirs, infused with the energy of the Violet Flame, offers a powerful way to harness these energies for healing both the physical and energetic bodies.

A crystal elixir is essentially water that has been charged with the vibrational energy of a particular crystal. Water is an excellent conductor of energy, and when it is exposed to the frequency of a crystal, it absorbs and retains that energy. When consumed or applied to the body, the elixir transmits the healing properties of the crystal to the individual. Adding the Violet Flame's energy into the process elevates the elixir's ability to cleanse, heal, and transmute negative energies, making it an even more potent tool for holistic healing.

Before preparing a crystal elixir, it's important to understand the energetic properties of different crystals and choose the ones that align with your healing intentions. Each crystal has its own vibrational frequency and is associated with specific healing properties. For example, amethyst is known for its protective and calming effects, making it an excellent choice for stress relief and spiritual connection. Rose quartz is linked to the heart chakra and is used to promote love, emotional healing, and compassion. Clear quartz, often called the "master healer," amplifies the energy of other crystals and is suitable for general healing purposes.

To begin, select a crystal that aligns with your healing goals. If your intention is to create an elixir for emotional healing, you might choose rose quartz. For spiritual protection or transmutation of negative energy, amethyst or black tourmaline may be more appropriate. Once you've selected the crystal, ensure that it is safe for water infusion, as some crystals can release toxic substances when submerged in water. Crystals such as selenite, malachite, and hematite should not be placed directly in water, as they can degrade or release harmful particles. In such cases, you can still use these crystals in elixirs by placing them near the water without direct contact, allowing their energy to infuse the water indirectly.

Once you've chosen a water-safe crystal, it's time to cleanse and charge it with both its natural energy and the energy of the Violet Flame. Begin by holding the crystal in your hands, taking a few deep breaths to center yourself. Visualize the Violet Flame surrounding the crystal, purifying it of any negative or stagnant energy it may have absorbed. As the flame burns around the crystal, repeat a decree such as: "I AM the Violet Flame, cleansing and purifying this crystal, filling it with divine love and healing energy." This step ensures that the crystal is energetically clear and ready to be charged with your intention.

Next, set your intention for the crystal elixir. Intentions are key in energy work, as they direct the flow of healing energy and focus it toward a specific goal. For example, if you are creating an elixir for emotional balance, you might set the intention that the elixir will help release feelings of sadness, fear, or anxiety, and replace them with peace and self-love. As you hold the crystal, silently or aloud state your intention, visualizing the crystal absorbing this energy.

Now you are ready to prepare the elixir. There are two main methods for infusing water with the energy of crystals: the direct method and the indirect method.

Direct Method: For the direct method, place the cleansed crystal directly into a glass or bowl of purified water. It's important to use a glass container, as plastic can interfere with the energy transmission. Place the container in a location where it will not be disturbed, ideally where it can be exposed to sunlight or moonlight to further charge the water with natural energy. Allow the crystal to sit in the water for several hours or overnight, giving the water ample time to absorb the crystal's vibrational energy.

Indirect Method: For crystals that are not safe to immerse in water, you can use the indirect method. In this case, place the crystal in a smaller glass or container, and then submerge that container within a larger bowl of water. The energy of the crystal will still infuse the water through the indirect contact. Alternatively, you can place the crystal beside or around the bowl of water, allowing its energy to resonate with the water without direct contact.

Once the water has been infused with the crystal's energy, it's time to invoke the Violet Flame to further charge the elixir. Hold the container of crystal-infused water in your hands and visualize the Violet Flame surrounding it, purifying and enhancing the healing properties of the elixir. You may repeat a decree such as: "I AM the Violet Flame, charging this elixir with divine healing and transmutation. May it purify and heal all who use it." As you hold this visualization, feel the energy of the Violet Flame merging with the crystal's vibration, creating a powerful healing elixir.

After the elixir has been fully charged, it can be used in a variety of ways. The most common method is to drink the elixir, taking small sips throughout the day to absorb the healing energy. When consuming the elixir, it's important to remain mindful of your intention, allowing the energy to integrate into your body and energy field. You may silently repeat your intention or a healing affirmation as you drink, such as: "As I drink this elixir, I absorb the energy of the Violet Flame and [crystal], bringing healing and balance to my body, mind, and spirit."

In addition to drinking the elixir, it can also be used topically. You can apply the elixir to specific areas of the body where healing is needed, such as over the heart chakra for emotional healing or the third eye for spiritual clarity. You might also anoint your wrists or temples with the elixir to bring its energy into your auric field throughout the day.

Another powerful use of crystal elixirs is in rituals or space clearing. You can sprinkle the elixir around your home, office, or healing space to purify the environment and raise its vibration. This is especially effective if you are working to cleanse a space of negative or stagnant energy, as the combination of the crystal's energy and the Violet Flame can transmute any discordant energies and restore harmony.

For longer-term storage, you can preserve your elixir by adding a few drops of a natural preservative, such as brandy or apple cider vinegar, to the water. Store the elixir in a glass bottle in a cool, dark place, and use it as needed over the following weeks or months. Be sure to periodically re-energize the elixir by holding it in your hands and charging it with the Violet Flame, especially if you are using it over an extended period.

Finally, crystal elixirs can also be incorporated into spiritual baths, enhancing the healing effects of water with the power of crystals and the Violet Flame. Simply add a few drops of the elixir to your bathwater and immerse yourself, allowing the energy to infuse your body and aura. As you soak, visualize the Violet Flame purifying your energy field and transmuting any negative or stagnant energy. This practice not only promotes physical relaxation but also provides a deep energetic cleansing, leaving you feeling refreshed and renewed.

In summary, crystal elixirs infused with the Violet Flame are a potent tool for holistic healing, offering a gentle yet powerful way to balance, heal, and protect the body, mind, and spirit. By combining the vibrational energy of crystals with the transmutational power of the Violet Flame, you create an elixir that supports deep healing on all levels. Whether used for drinking, anointing, space clearing, or spiritual baths, these elixirs are a versatile and effective addition to any healing practice.

Now that the basic process of creating crystal elixirs has been covered, the focus shifts to advanced techniques and specific applications of these elixirs in healing practices. Crystal elixirs, when combined with the Violet Flame, can address a variety of energetic imbalances and offer holistic support for physical, emotional, and spiritual healing. Understanding how to customize elixirs for specific purposes, how to work with different crystal combinations, and how to integrate the energy of the Violet Flame more deeply will enhance the effectiveness of these healing tools.

One of the key ways to increase the healing potency of a crystal elixir is by combining multiple crystals that work in harmony with each other. Each crystal resonates with a specific energy frequency, and combining them allows you to create elixirs that address multiple layers of healing. For example, if you are creating an elixir for emotional healing, you might combine rose quartz for love and compassion with amethyst for emotional balance and spiritual protection. The energy of the Violet Flame will enhance the transmutational aspect of the elixir, dissolving emotional pain and replacing it with higher frequencies of love and peace.

When combining crystals for an elixir, it is essential to choose stones that complement each other both energetically and practically. Be mindful of the compatibility of crystal energies, as some stones work together more effectively than others. For example, combining grounding stones like black tourmaline or hematite with higher vibration stones like clear quartz or amethyst creates a balance between grounding and spiritual elevation. If you're working with water-sensitive stones or those that should not be placed directly in water, remember to use the indirect method to ensure safety while still infusing the water with the stone's energy.

To create a multi-crystal elixir, follow the same steps as outlined, but use two or more crystals in the charging process. As you charge the elixir with each crystal, set a clear intention for how the combination of energies will work together. For example, if you are creating an elixir for protection and emotional resilience, your intention might be: "I ask the energy of black tourmaline and rose quartz, combined with the power of the Violet Flame, to protect my energy field and fill me with unconditional love." This clear intention helps to align the energies of the crystals with your healing goal, ensuring that the elixir is focused and powerful.

Once you have prepared your multi-crystal elixir, it can be used in the same ways as a single-crystal elixir—drinking it, applying it to the body, or using it for space clearing and rituals. However, multi-crystal elixirs tend to have a broader range of effects, so they are especially helpful when you are dealing with complex or layered issues that require multiple forms of energetic support.

In addition to combining crystals, you can also enhance the energy of a crystal elixir by charging it under specific celestial or planetary conditions. Both the moon and the sun emit powerful energetic frequencies that can influence the vibrational quality of an elixir. The most common practice is to charge elixirs under the light of the full moon, which amplifies the water's receptivity to energy. A full moon crystal elixir, charged with the Violet Flame, is particularly potent for emotional release, spiritual growth, and healing past traumas. Simply place your elixir outside or by a window where it can absorb the moonlight, and leave it overnight to charge.

Similarly, charging your elixir under the new moon is excellent for setting intentions for new beginnings, as the energy of the new moon supports manifestation and growth. In contrast, charging the elixir under the sun infuses it with vitality, clarity, and strength, making it ideal for physical healing and boosting energy. The combination of the sun's energy with the Violet Flame can help transmute fatigue, lethargy, and physical ailments, filling the body with renewed energy.

To work with celestial energy more deliberately, you might align your elixir preparation with planetary transits or astrological events. For example, charging an elixir during a lunar eclipse amplifies the transformative energy of the Violet Flame, helping to transmute deep-seated emotional patterns. You can also incorporate the energy of specific planets, such as charging an elixir during a Venus transit for love and relationship healing or during a Mars transit for courage and overcoming fear. Integrating these cosmic energies adds an extra layer of potency to the elixir, making it a highly versatile tool for both personal and collective healing.

Another advanced technique involves using sacred geometry and crystal grids to amplify the energy of the crystal elixir. Crystal grids are arrangements of crystals in specific geometric patterns, each shape carrying a unique energetic frequency. When combined with the Violet Flame, crystal grids can exponentially enhance the healing properties of an elixir by focusing and amplifying the energy in a targeted way.

To create a crystal grid for elixir preparation, select a geometric pattern that aligns with your intention. For healing, you might choose the flower of life or a circle to represent wholeness and unity. Lay the crystals in the chosen pattern around the water or elixir container, ensuring that each crystal is placed with intention. You can use quartz points to direct energy toward the water, or you can combine different crystals to create a more layered energetic effect. Once the grid is set, invoke the Violet Flame by visualizing the entire grid being surrounded by violet light, infusing both the crystals and the water with the flame's transformative energy.

Hold your hands over the grid and state your intention aloud, such as: "I invoke the energy of this crystal grid and the Violet Flame to charge this elixir with healing, protection, and transformation. May it bring peace and balance to all who use it." Allow the grid to sit undisturbed for several hours or overnight, giving the energy time to fully infuse the elixir.

Once the elixir is charged, it can be used in more targeted healing applications. For example, if you have created an elixir specifically for heart healing, you might use it in a heart chakra healing ritual. To do this, apply a few drops of the elixir directly to the heart center, visualizing the Violet Flame transmuting any grief, sadness, or emotional blockages. As you breathe in, imagine the energy of the elixir flowing into your heart, filling it with love, compassion, and healing light. You can repeat a decree such as: "I AM the Violet Flame, healing and opening my heart to unconditional love and joy."

Another powerful application of crystal elixirs is in distance healing. If you are working with someone who is not physically present, you can use the elixir as a conduit for sending healing energy across time and space. Simply hold the elixir in your hands, focusing on the person you are sending healing to. Visualize their energy field being surrounded by the Violet Flame, and mentally or verbally state your intention to send healing energy through the elixir. You might say: "I send the healing energy of the Violet Flame and this crystal elixir to [person's name], bringing peace, protection, and transformation to their body, mind, and spirit." As you hold this visualization, feel the energy of the elixir extending out to them, infusing their energy field with healing light.

For personal protection or energetic shielding, crystal elixirs infused with grounding and protective stones like black tourmaline, smoky quartz, or obsidian can be applied to the body, particularly on the solar plexus chakra or at the base of the spine. These areas are highly sensitive to energetic imbalances, and applying an elixir here helps to fortify your energy field against external influences. When combined with the Violet Flame, this protective barrier becomes even more potent, actively transmuting any lower energies that come into contact with your field.

Finally, crystal elixirs can be used as a tool for spiritual evolution and enhancing your connection to higher realms. By working with high-vibration crystals such as selenite, clear quartz, or celestite, you can create elixirs that support deeper meditative states, enhance intuition, and open the crown chakra and third eye. These elixirs, charged with the Violet Flame, help to clear mental fog, increase spiritual awareness, and bring clarity to your inner guidance. To use an elixir for this purpose, apply it to the third eye or crown chakra before meditation or spiritual practice, and visualize the Violet Flame activating these centers to bring divine wisdom and insight.

In conclusion, preparing crystal elixirs with the Violet Flame offers limitless potential for healing, protection, and spiritual growth. By integrating advanced techniques such as combining crystals, working with celestial energy, and using crystal grids, you create a more powerful healing tool that can be tailored to specific needs. Whether you are seeking emotional balance, physical healing, or spiritual awakening, these elixirs, when infused with the energy of the Violet Flame, provide a versatile and potent method for supporting your holistic journey.

Chapter 19
Healing Through Dreams and Spiritual Connection

Dreams have long been recognized as a gateway to deeper realms of the subconscious and a powerful tool for healing and spiritual connection. In holistic healing, dreams offer a unique avenue to access guidance from higher realms, receive healing messages, and work through emotional or energetic blockages that may not be accessible in waking life. By consciously working with dreams and invoking the energy of Saint Germain, individuals can deepen their healing process, gaining insights that promote transformation and spiritual growth.

At night, when the conscious mind rests, the subconscious is free to communicate more openly. This state allows for easier access to the realms where spiritual guides, including Saint Germain, can offer their wisdom and support. Dreams often reflect our unprocessed emotions, unresolved conflicts, and even karmic patterns from past lives. By learning to interpret and work with these dreams intentionally, we can bring greater clarity and healing into our lives.

The first step in using dreams for healing is to cultivate awareness of your dreams. Many people either do not remember their dreams or dismiss them as random, meaningless experiences. However, with practice, dream recall can be significantly improved. Before going to sleep, set a clear intention to remember your dreams. You can say something like: "I ask to remember my dreams tonight and receive clear messages for my healing and spiritual growth." Keep a journal by your bed, and upon waking, immediately write down any details you remember, even if they seem insignificant. Over time, you will begin to see patterns and themes emerge, offering insights into your healing process.

Working with the Violet Flame in dream states is a powerful way to transmute negative energies and heal emotional wounds. Before sleeping, take a few moments to center yourself and connect with the energy of Saint Germain and the Violet Flame. You can do this through a simple visualization. As you lie in bed, close your eyes and imagine the Violet Flame surrounding your body like a protective shield. This flame is dissolving any negative energy, emotional blocks, or fears that you may have accumulated throughout the day. Visualize the flame growing stronger and brighter, filling you with a sense of peace and safety.

Next, set a specific intention for your dream state. You might ask to receive guidance on a particular issue, heal a past trauma, or gain clarity on a relationship. For example, you can say: "I invoke the Violet Flame and the guidance of Saint Germain to assist me in my dreams tonight. Please help me heal [specific issue], transmute any negative energy related to this, and provide me with clear insights." This focused intention helps direct the energy of the dream, aligning it with your healing goals.

Dreams often communicate in the form of symbols and metaphors, which can be challenging to interpret at first. However, these symbolic messages are deeply personal and are often related to your subconscious mind's way of processing unresolved emotions or experiences. For instance, water in a dream may represent emotions, while being chased could symbolize a situation in waking life that you are avoiding. Over time, by journaling and reflecting on your dreams, you will develop a personal lexicon of dream symbols that you can use to decode their meaning.

If you find it difficult to understand the messages in your dreams, you can ask for clarification from your spiritual guides. Upon waking, sit quietly for a few moments and review the dream in your mind. Ask your guides or Saint Germain to help you understand the deeper meaning of the dream. Often, a new insight or interpretation will come to you in the form of an intuitive feeling, a thought, or even another dream the following night.

Sometimes, recurring dreams signal deep-seated issues that require more focused healing. For example, if you frequently dream of being lost, it may indicate a feeling of confusion or uncertainty in your waking life. In these cases, working with the Violet Flame in your dream practice can help dissolve the underlying emotional or karmic blocks that are manifesting through the dream. Each time you encounter the recurring dream, call upon the Violet Flame and visualize it transmuting the fear or confusion into clarity and peace.

For deeper spiritual connection, invoking Saint Germain before sleep can open the pathway for receiving direct guidance from the ascended master himself. Saint Germain, as a master of alchemy and spiritual transformation, often works with individuals during dream states to help them heal old wounds, release karmic patterns, and align with their higher purpose. To invoke his presence, you can use a decree before bed, such as: "Beloved Saint Germain, I call upon you to guide me in my dreams tonight. Help me to access the wisdom and healing I need for my highest good." As you drift off to sleep, imagine his presence beside you, guiding and protecting you throughout the night.

Sometimes, dreams may bring up unresolved emotional pain or past traumas that have not been fully processed in waking life. These dreams can be intense or even uncomfortable, but they offer an opportunity for deep healing. If you experience a dream that brings up fear, sadness, or other challenging emotions, do not shy away from it. Instead, see it as a message from your subconscious that these emotions are ready to be released and healed. Upon waking, you can work with the Violet Flame to continue the healing process. Visualize the emotions from the dream being bathed in violet light, allowing the flame to transmute them into love, forgiveness, or acceptance.

It is also possible to receive healing messages from spiritual guides in the form of direct communication during dreams. These messages may come from guides, ancestors, or even ascended masters like Saint Germain. In these dreams, you might have conversations with spiritual beings, receive symbolic gifts, or be shown scenes that reveal important insights about your path. If you experience such dreams, take note of the messages you receive, even if they don't make sense immediately. Often, these dream messages will unfold their meaning over time, offering guidance that helps you navigate your waking life.

Dreams can also provide a safe space for healing relationships, both past and present. If you are struggling with a difficult relationship, you might dream of interacting with the person in a way that allows you to express unresolved emotions or practice forgiveness. In these dreams, you have the opportunity to heal the energetic cords that bind you to the other person. After waking, you can use the Violet Flame to seal the healing by visualizing it dissolving any lingering negative energy between you and the other individual.

For those who feel drawn to lucid dreaming, where you become aware that you are dreaming and can consciously influence the dream's outcome, working with the Violet Flame offers even greater healing potential. In a lucid dream, you can call upon the Violet Flame to transmute negative energy within the dream itself, or you can ask for direct guidance from Saint Germain and your spiritual guides. Lucid dreaming requires practice and intention, but it allows for a more active role in your healing journey within the dream state.

Incorporating dream work into your holistic healing practice can significantly accelerate your spiritual growth and personal transformation. By paying attention to your dreams, invoking the Violet Flame, and calling upon the guidance of Saint Germain, you create a powerful synergy between your waking and sleeping states. This connection allows you to access higher wisdom, heal deep emotional wounds, and receive the guidance necessary to navigate your path with greater clarity and purpose.

Dreams are not just random occurrences but reflections of the deeper aspects of your soul. By engaging with them intentionally, you tap into a wellspring of healing and insight that supports your journey toward wholeness and alignment with your higher self. Through the Violet Flame and Saint Germain's guidance, your dreams become a sacred space for healing, transformation, and spiritual connection.

Building on the foundation of using dreams as a tool for healing and spiritual connection, the next step involves integrating practical techniques that deepen your ability to work with the energy of Saint Germain and the Violet Flame during the dream state. These practices will help you become more attuned to the messages and healing opportunities that arise in your dreams, as well as amplify your connection to higher realms of spiritual guidance.

One of the most effective ways to consciously engage with your dreams for healing is through pre-sleep rituals that align your energy and set clear intentions for the night ahead. These rituals prepare your subconscious mind to receive healing and guidance during sleep and create a sacred space for your spiritual work. A simple but powerful ritual begins with a few minutes of quiet meditation or deep breathing. As you settle your mind, visualize a protective sphere of violet light surrounding your body. This sphere acts as both a shield and a conduit for spiritual energy, ensuring that only positive, healing energies are able to enter your dream space.

Once you feel centered and connected to this protective energy, call upon Saint Germain and the Violet Flame. You might say: "Beloved Saint Germain, I ask for your guidance and protection as I sleep tonight. May the Violet Flame transmute any negative energy within me and my surroundings, and may my dreams bring healing, clarity, and spiritual insight." Setting this intention before sleep not only enhances the energy of your dreams but also invites the presence of Saint Germain to assist you in accessing higher realms of consciousness.

To further support the dream process, you can create a dream altar or sacred space near your bed. On this altar, place objects that represent healing, protection, and spiritual connection, such as crystals, a candle, or a picture of Saint Germain. Amethyst is an ideal crystal to include, as it enhances spiritual awareness and promotes restful sleep. You can also place a small glass of water on the altar to absorb healing energy throughout the night, which can be sipped upon waking to help integrate the energy of the dreams into your waking life.

Another valuable technique is the practice of dream incubation, where you focus on a specific question or issue you would like to explore in your dreams. Dream incubation is particularly helpful when you are seeking clarity on a challenge or when working through emotional or spiritual healing. Before going to bed, clearly state the question or issue you wish to resolve. For example, if you are struggling with a recurring emotional pattern, you might say: "I ask to receive insight and healing for my feelings of [name the emotion]. Please guide me to understand the source of this emotion and help me release it." As you fall asleep, visualize the Violet Flame surrounding the issue and transmuting any negative energy associated with it.

In the morning, upon waking, take a few moments to reflect on your dreams, even if they seem fragmented or unclear. Write down any symbols, emotions, or interactions that stood out. The more you practice this, the more you will notice recurring themes or patterns in your dreams, offering clues to the deeper healing that is taking place. Over time, the process of dream incubation becomes a dialogue between your conscious mind and your higher self, facilitated by the energy of the Violet Flame and Saint Germain.

For those seeking to develop their lucid dreaming abilities, incorporating the Violet Flame into your lucid dreams can lead to profound healing experiences. Lucid dreaming occurs when you become aware that you are dreaming while the dream is still happening, allowing you to take control of the dream's direction. To increase your chances of becoming lucid in a dream, practice reality checks throughout the day, asking yourself if you are dreaming and testing your environment for inconsistencies (such as trying to push your finger through your hand or checking if the time on a clock changes in an unrealistic way).

Once you become lucid in a dream, you can immediately call upon the Violet Flame for healing. Imagine the Violet Flame engulfing any negative or distressing aspects of the dream, transmuting fear or discomfort into light. This is particularly useful if you experience nightmares or difficult dream scenarios, as the Violet Flame can transform these experiences into opportunities for growth and healing. You can also ask for Saint Germain's guidance directly during a lucid dream, seeking advice or healing for specific issues in real time.

For example, if you find yourself in a dream scenario where you are feeling lost or confused, you can stop and ask Saint Germain for guidance. You might say: "Saint Germain, please show me the way forward," and then allow the dream to unfold with his presence and support. This can lead to surprising insights or emotional breakthroughs that continue to influence your waking life long after the dream has ended.

Another powerful use of dreams in healing is through ancestral healing. Dreams provide a bridge to connect with ancestral energies and resolve inherited emotional or karmic patterns. If you are aware of ancestral wounds or family dynamics that need healing, you can set the intention before sleep to work with these energies in your dreams. For example, you might ask: "I call upon the Violet Flame and Saint Germain to assist me in healing my ancestral lineage. Please help me release any karmic patterns or inherited wounds that are affecting my well-being." As you sleep, your dreams may reveal specific ancestors or family dynamics that need attention.

When you wake, reflect on the symbols or people that appeared in your dream and use the Violet Flame in your waking life to continue the healing process. You can visualize the flame surrounding your family line, dissolving any lingering negative energy and bringing peace and resolution to the past. This practice not only helps to heal ancestral patterns but also frees you from the influence of these patterns in your current life, allowing you to move forward with greater clarity and emotional freedom.

Healing relationships through dreams is another important aspect of this practice. If you are experiencing conflict or unresolved issues in a relationship, whether with a family member, friend, or partner, dreams offer a safe space to process and heal these emotions. Before bed, set the intention to work on healing the relationship in your dream state. You might say: "I ask the Violet Flame and Saint Germain to help me heal my relationship with [person's name]. Please show me how to release any negative energy and restore harmony."

During the dream, you may find yourself interacting with the person in question. Pay attention to how the dream unfolds—sometimes, the dream will offer you insights into the deeper emotional dynamics at play, or it may provide an opportunity to express feelings that you've been unable to share in waking life. After the dream, continue the healing by using the Violet Flame to transmute any remaining negative emotions or energetic cords between you and the person. Visualize the flame purifying the connection and filling it with love and light.

For deeper spiritual connection, consider using specific dream meditations before sleep that focus on opening the channels of communication with higher beings, including Saint Germain. One such meditation involves focusing on the crown chakra and the third eye, which are key centers for spiritual insight and higher consciousness. As you prepare for sleep, place your attention on your crown chakra at the top of your head and your third eye between your eyebrows. Visualize these centers being illuminated by the Violet Flame, gently opening to receive divine guidance.

As the light grows brighter, imagine a beam of violet light extending upward from your crown chakra, connecting you to the higher realms. Ask for guidance from Saint Germain and other spiritual beings aligned with your highest good. As you drift into sleep, trust that the insights you need will be delivered to you, either through direct messages in your dreams or as subtle impressions upon waking. Over time, this meditation will strengthen your connection to higher guidance, helping you to receive clearer, more profound messages in both your dreams and waking life.

Finally, dreams can serve as a platform for manifesting healing intentions in the physical world. If you are working on a specific healing goal, such as improving your physical health or overcoming an emotional challenge, you can use dreams to accelerate this process. Before sleep, focus on the desired outcome, whether it's healing a specific ailment or feeling more peaceful in your daily life. Visualize the outcome clearly in your mind and imagine the Violet Flame enveloping your body, assisting in the manifestation of your intention. Say an affirmation such as: "I am healed, whole, and aligned with divine health and peace."

As you sleep, your subconscious mind will work on aligning your energy with this intention, and you may receive symbolic dreams that reinforce your healing process. Upon waking, continue to focus on this intention, using the Violet Flame in your daily meditation or energy practices to support the manifestation of your goal.

In conclusion, the dream state offers an expansive and powerful arena for healing and spiritual connection. By working with the Violet Flame and invoking Saint Germain, you can use your dreams as a sacred space for transmuting negative energy, receiving guidance, and accelerating your spiritual growth. Through consistent practice, you will develop a deeper understanding of your subconscious patterns and unlock new levels of healing, clarity, and divine insight.

Chapter 20
Healing Ancestral and Inherited Patterns

Ancestral healing is a profound aspect of holistic spiritual work that focuses on clearing and transmuting the energetic patterns, traumas, and karmic debts inherited from our ancestors. These patterns can affect us deeply, even though they may not be immediately visible or consciously recognized. Working with the energy of the Violet Flame and the guidance of Saint Germain offers a powerful method for identifying and healing these ancestral influences, allowing us to free ourselves from limiting beliefs, emotional blockages, and recurring life patterns that may have been passed down through generations.

Many of the issues we face in life—whether emotional, mental, or physical—are not only a result of our own experiences but can be inherited through our family line. This inheritance includes not just genetic traits but also emotional and spiritual energy passed down from one generation to the next. For example, unhealed trauma, unresolved emotional pain, and karmic debts from our ancestors can become embedded in our own energy fields, manifesting as challenges or obstacles in our lives. These patterns may appear as chronic fears, relationship difficulties, financial struggles, or even physical ailments.

The first step in healing ancestral patterns is to become aware of them. This often requires reflecting on family history and identifying recurring themes or issues that seem to affect multiple generations. You might notice, for instance, a pattern of emotional repression, financial hardship, or strained relationships that has affected your parents, grandparents, and even earlier ancestors. Sometimes, these patterns are passed down unconsciously, and we may not immediately recognize their impact on our own lives.

As you begin this exploration, it's important to approach the process with compassion, both for yourself and for your ancestors. Ancestral healing is not about assigning blame or dwelling on past mistakes but about recognizing that unhealed energies can linger in the family line until they are consciously addressed. By working with the Violet Flame, you can release these energies, offering healing not only to yourself but to your entire ancestral line.

To begin healing ancestral patterns, you can invoke the Violet Flame and Saint Germain to guide and assist you. Create a sacred space where you feel grounded and connected to your spiritual practice. Light a candle or use crystals such as amethyst or black tourmaline to create a protective and healing atmosphere. Sit quietly, close your eyes, and take a few deep breaths. Visualize the Violet Flame surrounding you, cleansing your energy field and preparing you for the healing work ahead.

Once you feel centered, invite your ancestors into the space. You can say something like: "I call upon the wisdom and love of my ancestors. I invite you into this sacred space, and I offer my heart in service of healing and peace for our family line." As you say these words, imagine your ancestors gathering around you in a circle of light, each one offering their love and support for the healing process. You may or may not be aware of specific ancestors, but trust that those who are ready to assist in the healing will be present.

Next, bring your attention to the specific ancestral pattern you wish to heal. If you are unsure what pattern to focus on, you can ask Saint Germain and your ancestors to reveal the area of your life that most needs healing. Pay attention to any intuitive feelings, memories, or images that arise. This could be a recurring fear, a limiting belief, or an emotional block that feels deeply rooted. For example, you might recognize a pattern of fear around financial security, or you might sense unresolved grief that seems to have been passed down through the generations.

Once you have identified the pattern, visualize the Violet Flame surrounding it. See the flame moving through the pattern, dissolving any dense or negative energy associated with it. As the flame works its way through the energy, repeat a decree to invoke the transformative power of the Violet Flame. You might say: "I AM the Violet Flame, transmuting and healing all ancestral patterns of [name the pattern]. I release this energy from my family line and replace it with love, peace, and divine light."

As you hold this visualization, imagine the energy of the pattern being fully dissolved, leaving only light in its place. See the Violet Flame extending not only through your own energy field but also back through the generations, healing your ancestors and freeing them from the burden of this pattern. This is an important aspect of ancestral healing—by releasing the pattern from your own life, you also offer healing to those who came before you, allowing them to experience peace and resolution.

In some cases, ancestral patterns may be deeply ingrained, requiring multiple sessions of healing work. Be patient with the process, and know that each time you work with the Violet Flame, you are chipping away at the layers of accumulated energy. Over time, you may notice that the emotional intensity around the pattern begins to lessen, and you may experience a greater sense of freedom and empowerment in the area of your life that was previously affected.

Another aspect of ancestral healing involves working with karmic debts. Karmic debts are unresolved energies or lessons that have been passed down through generations, often as a result of actions or decisions made by your ancestors. These karmic debts can manifest as repeating life circumstances, such as recurring financial difficulties, relationship struggles, or health issues, which seem to follow the family line. By addressing and healing these karmic debts, you can release the hold they have on your present life and future generations.

To begin healing karmic debts, set the intention to release any unresolved karma from your ancestral line. You can say: "I call upon the Violet Flame and the guidance of Saint Germain to help me release any karmic debts inherited from my ancestors. May these debts be transmuted and healed, freeing me and my family from their influence." Visualize the Violet Flame moving through your energy field, dissolving any karmic imprints or attachments. You may also visualize the flame moving through the energy field of your ancestors, releasing them from the karmic cycles they have carried.

In addition to working with the Violet Flame, forgiveness is a key element of ancestral healing. Many of the patterns we inherit are linked to unresolved emotional wounds or conflicts between family members. By practicing forgiveness, you can release the emotional charge associated with these wounds and allow healing to take place. Begin by offering forgiveness to your ancestors for any actions or decisions that contributed to the patterns you are healing. You might say: "I forgive my ancestors for any harm or suffering that has been passed down through our family line. I release this energy with love and compassion."

Next, offer forgiveness to yourself for any role you may have played in perpetuating these patterns, whether consciously or unconsciously. Forgiving yourself is just as important as forgiving your ancestors, as it frees you from feelings of guilt or shame that may have been inherited along with the patterns. Say: "I forgive myself for carrying this ancestral pattern. I release all guilt, shame, and fear, and I embrace my role as a healer for myself and my family."

As you work with forgiveness and the Violet Flame, you may feel a deep sense of emotional release. It is not uncommon for emotions such as grief, anger, or sadness to arise during ancestral healing, as you are clearing energy that may have been buried for generations. Allow these emotions to flow through you without judgment, knowing that they are part of the healing process. You can use the Violet Flame to transmute these emotions, visualizing them being absorbed into the flame and transformed into light.

Over time, as you continue to heal ancestral patterns and karmic debts, you may notice a shift not only in your own life but also in the lives of your family members. While each person's healing journey is unique, the energetic work you do for yourself can have a ripple effect on the entire family line, offering healing to those who may not even be consciously aware of it. This is the beauty of ancestral healing—it not only frees you from the burdens of the past but also creates a path of healing for future generations.

In summary, healing ancestral and inherited patterns is a profound and transformative process that allows you to release the energetic imprints of the past, freeing yourself and your family from limiting beliefs, emotional wounds, and karmic debts. By working with the Violet Flame and the guidance of Saint Germain, you can transmute these patterns and create a new foundation of healing, love, and peace for yourself and your descendants. Through this work, you honor your ancestors, heal the present, and pave the way for a brighter future.

As we continue the journey of healing ancestral and inherited patterns, the focus now shifts toward practical techniques for deeper healing and the ongoing maintenance of a clear energetic connection between you and your ancestral line. Ancestral healing is not a one-time event; it is an ongoing process that requires continuous attention and care, much like tending to a garden. By integrating specific rituals, decrees, and meditations into your spiritual practice, you can continue to release inherited energies, cultivate healing across generations, and prevent old patterns from re-emerging.

One powerful practice for ancestral healing is the use of decrees in combination with the Violet Flame. Decrees, which are spoken affirmations infused with spiritual intention, can be directed specifically toward healing the family line. These decrees help to channel the energy of the Violet Flame into areas of ancestral trauma or karmic debt, dissolving the patterns at their root and restoring balance and harmony.

A simple but effective decree for ancestral healing might be: "I AM the Violet Flame, transmuting all ancestral patterns of limitation, fear, and separation in my family line. I release these patterns from my life and the lives of my ancestors, freeing us to live in peace, love, and divine truth." As you repeat this decree, visualize the Violet Flame moving through your body and extending back through your ancestral line. Imagine it burning away any dense or stagnant energy, leaving only light and healing in its place.

For more specific issues, you can tailor the decree to focus on particular patterns you have identified within your family. For example, if your family has a history of financial struggle, you might say: "I AM the Violet Flame, transmuting all patterns of poverty, lack, and limitation from my family line. I release these energies and restore the flow of abundance, prosperity, and divine wealth to myself and my ancestors." Repeating this decree daily, or as often as you feel guided, will gradually dissolve the energetic blocks that have been passed down and open the way for new, more positive experiences to flow into your life.

Another key practice in ancestral healing is creating a dedicated space where you can connect with your ancestors and work with the energy of the Violet Flame. This space could be a small altar or a quiet corner in your home where you feel comfortable and at peace. On your altar, you may place objects that symbolize your connection to your family and heritage, such as photographs of loved ones, heirlooms, or mementos that carry ancestral energy. You can also place crystals that support ancestral work, such as black tourmaline for protection, rose quartz for love and emotional healing, and clear quartz for clarity and amplification of energy.

Once you have set up your sacred space, spend time there regularly in meditation and reflection. Begin by lighting a candle or incense to honor your ancestors, calling upon them to join you in this space for healing. You might say: "I honor and welcome my ancestors, known and unknown, to this sacred space. I ask for your guidance and support as we work together to heal the patterns of our lineage." As you sit quietly, allow any intuitive impressions or memories to arise, trusting that your ancestors are communicating with you in the way that is most appropriate for your healing journey.

During these meditative sessions, you can focus on a specific ancestral issue that you wish to heal. For example, if there is a pattern of unresolved grief in your family, visualize the Violet Flame surrounding the energy of that grief, transmuting it into peace and acceptance. You may also feel guided to speak to your ancestors directly, offering them forgiveness or asking for their forgiveness in return. Many ancestral wounds stem from unspoken words or unresolved emotions, and by bringing these feelings into the light, you allow them to be healed.

It is also important to recognize that ancestral healing can extend beyond your bloodline. Many of the patterns we carry are influenced not only by our direct ancestors but also by the collective energies of the communities, cultures, and even nations we are part of. Collective trauma—such as war, colonization, systemic oppression, or environmental devastation—often leaves deep energetic imprints that affect entire populations and can be passed down through generations. These collective wounds, while not specific to your family, still impact the way you experience life, relationships, and spirituality.

In cases where you sense that a collective pattern is influencing your life, you can expand your ancestral healing work to include the broader community. Begin by setting the intention to heal not just your personal family line, but also the collective energies that have contributed to the issue. For instance, if you are working to heal a pattern of fear or separation that stems from a history of war or displacement, you might say: "I invoke the Violet Flame to heal the collective wounds of war and separation. I release the energy of fear, anger, and division from my ancestral line and from the collective consciousness. May the Violet Flame restore peace, unity, and love to all beings."

This practice of collective healing is particularly powerful during times of global or societal upheaval, as it helps to transmute the dense energies of fear and separation that often arise during these periods. By working with the Violet Flame in this way, you are not only healing your own ancestral patterns but also contributing to the healing of the broader human family. This work is aligned with Saint Germain's teachings on planetary healing, which emphasize the interconnectedness of all beings and the importance of transmuting collective energies to raise the vibration of the Earth.

As you continue to engage in ancestral healing, you may notice that certain patterns or emotions resurface periodically, even after you have worked to clear them. This is natural, as ancestral healing often occurs in layers. Each time a pattern resurfaces, it offers an opportunity to address it from a deeper level, clearing out the remaining energy that was not fully healed in previous sessions. Rather than becoming discouraged, see these moments as part of the ongoing process of spiritual growth and transformation.

To support yourself during these times, it is helpful to engage in self-care rituals that keep your energy grounded and clear. Regular energy cleansing practices, such as bathing with salt and herbs, spending time in nature, or using crystals to balance your energy field, can help you maintain a sense of peace and stability as you work through the deeper layers of ancestral healing. You may also find it beneficial to incorporate movement into your healing process, such as yoga, tai chi, or dance, to release any stagnant energy from the body and promote the free flow of life force.

Ancestral healing is a profound and sacred responsibility, and it is important to honor both yourself and your ancestors throughout this journey. As you release old patterns and transmute dense energies, you create a pathway for greater light, love, and healing to flow through your family line. This work not only benefits you but also has a ripple effect, bringing healing to your ancestors, your descendants, and the collective consciousness of humanity.

In closing, remember that you are never alone in this process. The guidance and protection of Saint Germain, the Violet Flame, and your ancestors are always available to you as you engage in this transformative work. Through patience, compassion, and dedication, you can heal the patterns of the past and open the way for a future of peace, joy, and spiritual fulfillment—for yourself and for those who will come after you.

Chapter 21
Harmonizing Your Relationship with Money and Abundance

The relationship between money, abundance, and spiritual energy is deeply interconnected. Many people carry subconscious beliefs about money that block the natural flow of abundance in their lives, whether due to personal experiences, societal conditioning, or inherited patterns from their family line. In holistic healing, understanding and harmonizing your relationship with money is essential for living a balanced and fulfilled life. The teachings of Saint Germain and the Violet Flame offer powerful tools for transmuting limiting beliefs around wealth and prosperity, opening the door to a greater flow of abundance on all levels—material, emotional, and spiritual.

Money is often viewed purely in terms of its material aspects, but from a spiritual perspective, it is simply another form of energy exchange. Like all energy, money must flow freely in order to be in harmony. When fear, scarcity, or guilt are attached to money, it blocks the natural flow of abundance. These emotions often manifest as financial struggles, a sense of lack, or a feeling of unworthiness to receive wealth. By healing the energetic blocks around money, you can restore the flow of abundance in your life, aligning yourself with a higher frequency of prosperity that is based on trust, balance, and gratitude.

To begin harmonizing your relationship with money, it's important to first identify the beliefs you hold about wealth and abundance. Many of these beliefs are subconscious and may have been formed in childhood, based on your family's attitudes toward money. Reflect on your early experiences with money— what did your parents or caregivers teach you about it, either directly or indirectly? Were there messages of fear or scarcity, such as "money doesn't grow on trees" or "we can't afford that"? Or perhaps there were mixed signals about money being something desirable yet shameful to talk about.

As you reflect, make a list of the most prominent beliefs or emotions that come up around money. These might include feelings of guilt about having more than others, fear of not having enough, or a belief that money is inherently bad or corrupting. Once you've identified these beliefs, the next step is to release them using the power of the Violet Flame.

Find a quiet space where you can meditate without distraction. Close your eyes and take a few deep breaths, centering yourself in the present moment. Visualize the Violet Flame surrounding you, gently purifying your energy field. As you breathe deeply, bring your awareness to the limiting belief or emotion you want to release. For example, you might focus on the belief that "money is scarce" or the fear of "not having enough." Hold this belief in your mind's eye, and then visualize the Violet Flame enveloping it, transmuting the dense energy into light. As the flame burns away the belief, repeat a decree such as: "I AM the Violet Flame, transmuting all fear, scarcity, and limitation around money. I release these beliefs and open myself to the flow of divine abundance."

As you work with the Violet Flame to clear these beliefs, be gentle with yourself. Limiting beliefs around money can be deeply ingrained, and it may take time to fully release them. Trust that each time you work with the Violet Flame, you are dissolving another layer of resistance, bringing yourself closer to a state of alignment with the energy of abundance.

Once you've begun to clear limiting beliefs, it's important to replace them with positive affirmations that align with the flow of abundance. Affirmations are a powerful tool for reprogramming your subconscious mind, shifting your thoughts and energy toward a more prosperous mindset. Choose affirmations that resonate with you and reflect the new beliefs you wish to cultivate. Some examples might include:

"I am worthy of receiving abundance in all forms."

"Money flows to me easily and effortlessly."
"I am a magnet for divine prosperity and wealth."
"The more I give, the more I receive in perfect balance."

Repeat these affirmations daily, either in meditation or throughout the day, allowing them to take root in your consciousness. As you do, notice how your relationship with money begins to shift—whether through small changes in your financial situation, an increase in unexpected opportunities, or a deeper sense of peace around your finances.

A key aspect of harmonizing your relationship with money is learning to see abundance in all areas of your life, not just financially. Abundance is a state of being, a frequency that can be experienced in every aspect of existence—from the love in your relationships to the beauty of nature, to the opportunities for growth and learning that present themselves each day. By cultivating gratitude for the abundance you already have, you raise your vibration and align more fully with the flow of prosperity.

To practice this, start each day by listing three things you are grateful for that bring abundance into your life. These could be as simple as the warmth of the sun, the love of a friend or family member, or the joy of creative expression. The more you acknowledge the abundance that already surrounds you, the more you attract. Gratitude is a magnet for abundance, and when you focus on what you have, rather than what you lack, you naturally draw more of it into your life.

In addition to shifting your mindset, it's also important to take practical actions that support the flow of money in your life. Money, like any form of energy, must be circulated in order to flow freely. This means being mindful of both how you give and how you receive. If you have a habit of hoarding money out of fear, try loosening your grip by giving freely to causes or people you care about. This doesn't mean giving away more than you can afford, but rather cultivating a spirit of generosity, trusting that what you give will return to you multiplied.

At the same time, practice receiving with gratitude. Many people struggle with the energy of receiving, often feeling unworthy of the gifts or opportunities that come their way. If you find it difficult to accept help, gifts, or compliments, begin by consciously practicing the art of receiving. When someone offers you a gift, a compliment, or assistance, take a moment to fully receive it, acknowledging it with gratitude. You can even visualize the Violet Flame surrounding the energy of the gift, ensuring that it is in alignment with your highest good.

As you continue to harmonize your relationship with money, you may also feel called to explore the spiritual dimensions of wealth. In the teachings of Saint Germain, wealth is seen not as a goal in itself but as a tool for fulfilling your divine purpose. Money is a form of energy that can be used to support your mission on Earth, whether that involves creating art, starting a business, helping others, or pursuing a path of spiritual development. When you align your financial goals with your higher purpose, money flows naturally and effortlessly, supporting you in fulfilling your soul's calling.

One way to align your financial life with your spiritual path is by setting the intention to use your wealth for the highest good of all. You can make a daily practice of affirming: "I use my wealth and abundance for the highest good, in alignment with my divine purpose." This affirmation reminds you that money is not an end in itself but a means of creating positive change in the world. Whether through acts of charity, supporting sustainable practices, or using your resources to pursue your own spiritual development, money becomes a tool for greater good when it is aligned with divine purpose.

It's essential to trust the process of transformation. As you clear limiting beliefs, embrace the flow of abundance, and align your financial life with your spiritual purpose, you may experience fluctuations in your financial circumstances. Trust that these fluctuations are part of the natural ebb and flow of energy, and remain focused on the greater picture of prosperity that you are cultivating. By working with the Violet Flame and Saint

Germain, you are transforming not just your relationship with money but also your understanding of wealth as a divine energy that flows through all aspects of life.

In summary, harmonizing your relationship with money and abundance is about much more than financial gain. It's about clearing the energetic blocks that prevent you from fully receiving the prosperity that is your birthright and learning to view money as a tool for spiritual growth and service. Through the transformative power of the Violet Flame and the guidance of Saint Germain, you can release limiting beliefs, align with the flow of abundance, and use your wealth for the highest good, creating a life of balance, joy, and fulfillment.

After laying the foundation of recognizing and releasing limiting beliefs around money, it's time to move into the practical application of spiritual principles to cultivate a deeper and lasting flow of abundance in your life. Abundance is not just about financial wealth—it encompasses health, love, opportunities, creativity, and overall well-being.

One of the most essential aspects of living in abundance is to embody the energy of abundance. Embodying abundance means not just thinking positively about money and prosperity but truly feeling and living as if abundance is already present in your life. This creates a vibrational match to the frequency of prosperity, attracting more of it into your experience. To cultivate this mindset, it's crucial to shift your focus from lack to gratitude, celebrating even the smallest expressions of abundance in your daily life.

One way to embody the energy of abundance is by engaging in rituals of gratitude. Begin your day by focusing on what you are grateful for in every area of your life. Take a few moments to write down three to five things you are thankful for, specifically related to wealth and abundance. These could include anything from a steady paycheck, a supportive community, opportunities to grow in your career, or even access to resources that help you achieve your goals. Gratitude is a potent energetic signal that affirms your trust in the universe's ability to provide for you, enhancing your magnetic power to draw more of what you need.

A helpful technique to reinforce this mindset is a prosperity journal. Each day, write down any experience or manifestation of abundance that comes your way—whether it's a small financial gain, a gift, a generous opportunity, or even an unexpected discount. By recording these signs of prosperity, you shift your focus away from scarcity and build a narrative of abundance in your life. Over time, you will begin to notice that the more you focus on the wealth that already surrounds you, the more you attract.

Another important practice is working with decrees and affirmations that specifically address financial flow and prosperity. Using the Violet Flame in these affirmations can further amplify their power, as the Flame transmutes any remaining fear, doubt, or blocks that might still linger in your energy field. To do this, visualize the Violet Flame surrounding you as you speak your affirmations aloud, infusing each statement with light and transformative power. Here are some affirmations you can incorporate into your daily practice:

"I AM the Violet Flame, transmuting all fear and doubt around wealth. I now open myself fully to the flow of abundance."

"I AM aligned with divine prosperity, and money flows to me easily and effortlessly."

"I trust in the infinite abundance of the universe, and I am open to receiving all forms of wealth, health, and happiness."

"I AM the Violet Flame, dissolving all patterns of scarcity. I am a magnet for divine wealth and prosperity."

Repeating these affirmations daily, especially during your morning meditation or before going to bed, will reinforce the energetic shifts you are making and help you maintain a high vibrational frequency that is in harmony with abundance.

In addition to working with affirmations, you can use visualization techniques to further enhance your connection to the flow of wealth. Visualization is a powerful tool for manifesting your desires, as it allows you to align your thoughts, emotions, and energy with the reality you wish to create. Spend a few moments each day visualizing yourself living in a state of complete abundance—this could mean seeing yourself in a thriving career, surrounded by loving relationships, or experiencing financial freedom. As you visualize, focus not only on the images but also on the feelings of joy, gratitude, and ease that come with being in a state of prosperity.

To take this a step further, use the Violet Flame in your visualizations to transmute any negative energy or limiting beliefs that may still arise. For example, if you are visualizing financial abundance but feel doubt or fear creeping in, imagine the Violet Flame burning away those feelings, leaving only light and positivity. You can also imagine the Violet Flame flowing through your financial situation, clearing away any blockages in the flow of money and replacing them with the energy of abundance and growth.

Another key element of attracting and maintaining abundance is to clear your physical and energetic space. Often, clutter in your home or workspace can reflect and contribute to energetic stagnation, blocking the flow of prosperity. Take some time to declutter your environment, especially areas related to your finances—such as your wallet, office, or any space where you handle money. Clear out old papers, organize your belongings, and create a space that feels open and welcoming to new energy.

As you declutter, call upon the Violet Flame to assist in clearing any energetic residue that may be tied to fear, lack, or old financial struggles. For example, as you clean your workspace, visualize the Violet Flame sweeping through the area, dissolving any negative energy and filling the space with the light of abundance. This not only creates a more harmonious physical environment but also aligns your energy with prosperity.

In addition to clearing your space, you can also engage in rituals of financial flow. One simple but powerful practice is to create a money altar. This altar serves as a focal point for your intentions around wealth and abundance. On this altar, place symbols of prosperity, such as coins, crystals associated with wealth (like citrine, pyrite, or green aventurine), and affirmations or images that represent your financial goals. Light a candle each day at this altar, and as you do, affirm your connection to the flow of divine wealth.

You can also place a bowl of coins or bills on your money altar as a symbol of financial abundance. Each time you place money in the bowl, say a prayer or affirmation that acknowledges the infinite supply of money available to you. For example, you might say: "I bless this money and all money that flows into my life. I give thanks for the abundance I receive, knowing that it is a reflection of the divine flow of prosperity." This ritual helps to reinforce the belief that money is a form of energy that flows to you and from you in harmony with universal laws.

Another powerful exercise is to give with intention. Generosity is a key aspect of abundance because it acknowledges that there is more than enough for everyone. When you give to others—whether through charitable donations, offering your time and resources, or simply sharing a meal with someone—you affirm your trust in the flow of abundance. However, it's important to give from a place of love and gratitude rather than obligation or guilt. Before giving, take a moment to bless the gift with the Violet Flame, saying: "I give freely and joyfully, knowing that I am always supported by the infinite flow of abundance."

A critical aspect of maintaining abundance is learning to release control and trust the universe. While it's important to take practical steps toward financial stability and wealth, it's equally important to release any attachment to the outcome. True abundance flows when we trust that the universe is always providing for us in ways that may not always be immediately visible. When you find yourself worrying about money or feeling anxious about your financial future, use the Violet Flame to transmute those feelings into peace and surrender. You might say: "I trust the universe to provide for all my needs. I release all fear and doubt and open myself fully to the divine flow of abundance."

Trusting the process of manifestation is about recognizing that abundance may come in unexpected forms. Sometimes, the flow of wealth may not be purely financial but may arrive as support, opportunities, or unexpected gifts. By keeping your heart and mind open to all forms of prosperity, you allow the universe to surprise you with blessings beyond your expectations.

In summary, cultivating a harmonious relationship with money and abundance requires both an inner shift in consciousness and practical steps that align you with the energy of prosperity. By working with the Violet Flame to clear limiting beliefs, embracing gratitude, practicing affirmations and visualizations, and engaging in rituals that support financial flow, you can transform your relationship with wealth and attract greater abundance into your life. Through trust, generosity, and alignment with your divine purpose, you open the door to a life of balance, joy, and true prosperity, grounded in spiritual abundance.

Chapter 22
Healing Chronic Illnesses with the Violet Flame

Chronic illnesses are deeply rooted in a person's physical, emotional, and spiritual being. From the holistic perspective of healing taught by Saint Germain, illness is not only a physical condition but also the result of energetic imbalances that manifest in the body over time. These imbalances may be caused by unresolved emotional trauma, persistent negative thought patterns, karmic influences, or blocked spiritual energy. Chronic illnesses, therefore, require healing on multiple levels to address the underlying causes and restore the flow of vital energy.

The Violet Flame is a powerful tool for transmuting the energetic causes of chronic illnesses, working beyond the physical symptoms to reach the deeper levels of consciousness where these imbalances originate. The Violet Flame operates by clearing dense, stagnant energy from the auric field and energy centers, allowing the body's natural healing processes to activate and function more effectively.

Before working with the Violet Flame for chronic illness, it is essential to understand that healing is a holistic process. While the physical body is the most obvious aspect of illness, the energetic, mental, and emotional layers of a person's being are equally important. Healing chronic illness requires addressing the energetic roots of the condition, which often lie in unhealed emotions, long-held negative beliefs, or karmic patterns that have been carried over from past lives. The Violet Flame, with its transformative power, is uniquely suited to dissolve these blockages and restore the flow of divine energy throughout the body and spirit.

To begin using the Violet Flame for chronic illness, the first step is to identify the energetic root cause of the condition.

This requires introspection and a willingness to explore not just the physical symptoms but also the emotional and spiritual aspects of the illness. You may want to ask yourself: What emotions are tied to this illness? Are there recurring thoughts or fears associated with it? Have I experienced any significant life events or traumas that may have contributed to the development of this condition? By reflecting on these questions, you can start to uncover the underlying energetic patterns that are contributing to the illness.

Once you have a clearer sense of the emotional or spiritual roots of the illness, it is time to invoke the Violet Flame for healing. Begin by creating a sacred space where you can focus fully on the healing process. Light a candle or use crystals such as amethyst, which is aligned with the energy of the Violet Flame, to enhance the healing atmosphere. Sit comfortably and take a few deep breaths, allowing your mind and body to relax. Visualize the Violet Flame surrounding you, its gentle purple light purifying your energy field and dissolving any negativity or tension.

As you meditate on the Violet Flame, focus your attention on the area of your body that is affected by the illness. Visualize the Violet Flame entering that part of your body, gently burning away any dense or stagnant energy that may be contributing to the condition. You can also use your hands to direct the energy, placing them over the affected area and imagining the healing energy of the Violet Flame flowing through your hands into your body. As the energy moves through you, repeat a healing decree to amplify the power of the Violet Flame. You might say: "I AM the Violet Flame, transmuting all disease, pain, and imbalance from my body. I release this illness and restore the flow of divine health and vitality."

It's important to remain patient and compassionate with yourself during this process. Chronic illness often develops over a long period of time, and healing can take time as well. The Violet Flame works on multiple levels of your being, so while you may not see immediate results in the physical body, trust that healing is occurring at the energetic and spiritual levels. As you continue to work with the Violet Flame, you may notice shifts in your emotional or mental state, such as a release of old fears or an increased sense of peace and well-being. These shifts are signs that the deeper layers of the illness are being addressed, even before the physical symptoms begin to change.

In addition to using the Violet Flame for direct healing, it is also beneficial to engage in practices that support the body's natural healing processes. This might include meditation, energy healing, or gentle physical movement, such as yoga or tai chi, to keep the body's energy flowing. It is also important to pay attention to your diet, rest, and overall lifestyle, as these factors play a significant role in supporting the healing journey. The Violet Flame can enhance and accelerate these practices, but it is important to approach healing from a holistic perspective, addressing the physical, emotional, and spiritual aspects of your being.

Another powerful tool in the healing process is the practice of forgiveness, both toward yourself and others. Chronic illnesses are often associated with long-held emotional wounds or unresolved conflicts, which can create energetic blockages in the body. By practicing forgiveness, you release the emotional weight that may be contributing to the illness, freeing your energy to flow more freely. Begin by forgiving yourself for any judgments or guilt you may be holding around the illness. You might say: "I forgive myself for any role I may have played in creating this illness. I release all guilt, shame, and fear, and I open myself to the flow of healing love and light."

Next, extend forgiveness to others who may be connected to the emotional or spiritual roots of the illness. This could include forgiving family members, friends, or even societal influences that may have contributed to the development of the condition. As you practice forgiveness, visualize the Violet Flame dissolving any cords or attachments between you and the other person, allowing both of you to be free of the past and move forward in peace.

In addition to forgiveness, working with positive affirmations can help to reprogram the mind and body toward healing. Chronic illnesses are often accompanied by patterns of negative thinking, such as fear, worry, or hopelessness. These thought patterns can reinforce the illness and make it more difficult to heal. By consciously choosing positive affirmations, you can begin to shift your mindset toward health and vitality. Some affirmations you might use include:

"I am whole, healthy, and full of vitality."

"My body is capable of healing itself with the support of divine energy."

"I am open to receiving the healing power of the Violet Flame."

"Every cell in my body is being restored to perfect health."

Repeat these affirmations daily, particularly during moments when you feel discouraged or overwhelmed by the illness. As you speak these words, visualize the Violet Flame surrounding your body, reinforcing the energy of health and dissolving any remaining negativity.

Finally, it is important to remember that healing is not just about the absence of illness but about creating a state of holistic balance and well-being. This means not only addressing the symptoms of the illness but also creating a life that supports your overall health—physically, emotionally, mentally, and spiritually. As you work with the Violet Flame to heal chronic illness, consider how you can bring more balance into your life. Are there areas where you are overextended or out of alignment with your true self? Are there emotional patterns or beliefs that no longer serve you? By addressing these questions, you can create a foundation of health that goes beyond simply managing symptoms and moves toward true healing and transformation.

In conclusion, the Violet Flame offers a powerful and compassionate tool for healing chronic illnesses, addressing not only the physical symptoms but also the deeper energetic and spiritual causes. Through meditation, visualization, forgiveness, and positive affirmations, you can work with the transformative energy of the Violet Flame to release the blocks that contribute to illness and restore the flow of divine health throughout your being. Healing is a journey, and by approaching it with patience, trust, and a commitment to holistic well-being, you can experience profound transformation on all levels of your existence.

Building on the foundations laid, this section delves deeper into the practical techniques for using the Violet Flame to heal chronic illnesses, offering specific exercises, visualizations, and decrees to apply in your healing practice. Chronic illness often requires sustained, focused effort to shift the energetic patterns that have contributed to the condition. By consistently working with the Violet Flame and the guidance of Saint Germain, you can achieve greater clarity, healing, and ultimately transformation.

One of the most effective ways to use the Violet Flame for chronic illness is to create a daily ritual dedicated to your healing process. This ritual can be as simple or elaborate as you feel comfortable with, but the key is consistency. By engaging in this practice regularly, you build momentum in the healing process, allowing the transformative energy of the Violet Flame to work through all layers of your being. Below is a suggested outline for a daily healing ritual that you can adapt to suit your personal needs:

Prepare Your Space: Begin by creating a peaceful and sacred environment where you can focus on your healing. Light a candle and place crystals such as amethyst or clear quartz around you to amplify the energy. You might also choose to play soft, meditative music to enhance the calming atmosphere.

Ground Yourself: Sit in a comfortable position and close your eyes. Take a few deep breaths, inhaling through your nose and exhaling through your mouth. As you breathe, imagine roots extending from the base of your spine into the Earth, grounding you deeply. Feel the Earth's energy rise through your body, anchoring you in the present moment.

Invoke the Violet Flame: Visualize the Violet Flame surrounding you, gently purifying your energy field. As you breathe, feel the flame entering your body, moving through every cell, organ, and tissue. Imagine it dissolving any negative energy, stagnation, or illness that may be present in your body. You can enhance this visualization by repeating a decree such as: "I AM the Violet Flame, dissolving all imbalance, illness, and disease in my body. I transmute all dense energy into light and restore the flow of divine health."

Focus on the Affected Area: Direct the Violet Flame to the specific area of your body that is affected by chronic illness. For example, if you are dealing with chronic pain in your joints, visualize the Violet Flame moving through your joints, transmuting the pain into light. If you are healing a chronic respiratory condition, imagine the Violet Flame purifying your lungs, filling them with vibrant energy. As you do this, feel the tension, pain, or discomfort melting away, replaced by a sense of lightness and vitality.

Speak Your Healing Decrees: After visualizing the healing energy in the affected area, speak decrees aloud to reinforce the healing process. For example:

"I AM the Violet Flame, healing my body at all levels."

"I command the energy of perfect health to flow through me now."

"I release all energy patterns that no longer serve my highest good." As you repeat these decrees, imagine them creating ripples of light that move through your entire body, expanding outward and filling your auric field with healing energy.

Express Gratitude: Once you have completed the healing visualization and decrees, take a moment to express gratitude for the healing that has taken place. You might say: "Thank you, Violet Flame, for transmuting all imbalance and restoring my health. I trust in the divine healing process." Feel the gratitude deeply in your heart and let it radiate outward, affirming your faith in the ongoing healing journey.

Close the Ritual: After completing your healing session, gently bring your awareness back to your breath. Take a few moments to ground yourself once more, feeling your connection to the Earth. You can choose to journal any thoughts, insights, or shifts in energy that you experienced during the ritual, helping to track your healing progress.

In addition to this daily practice, longer meditative sessions with the Violet Flame can deepen your healing process. These extended sessions allow you to explore the emotional and mental layers associated with chronic illness, offering more profound insights into the patterns that need to be released. A guided meditation focused on healing might begin by centering yourself and visualizing the Violet Flame surrounding your entire body. As you settle into a relaxed state, invite memories or emotions related to the illness to come forward. Trust that whatever arises is part of the healing process, even if it brings up discomfort.

As these emotions or memories surface, bring the Violet Flame into them. For example, if an old trauma or unresolved conflict appears in your awareness, visualize the Violet Flame surrounding it, burning away the pain and leaving only peace in its place. You can also ask for guidance from Saint Germain or your spiritual guides to assist you in understanding the root cause of these emotions. By doing this, you are not only addressing the physical symptoms of the illness but also healing the emotional wounds that may be contributing to the condition.

In many cases, chronic illnesses are tied to karmic patterns carried over from past lives. These patterns can manifest as persistent physical symptoms, emotional blockages, or limiting beliefs that seem resistant to healing. The Violet Flame is an especially powerful tool for transmuting karmic energy, as it works on the soul level to dissolve negative karmic ties and release the individual from the cycle of suffering. If you suspect that your chronic illness may have karmic origins, consider engaging in a meditation specifically focused on clearing karmic energy.

In this meditation, you would once again invoke the Violet Flame, asking it to transmute any karmic patterns related to the illness. As you meditate, visualize the Violet Flame traveling back through your soul's timeline, moving through past lives and dissolving any karmic debts or unresolved energy that may be affecting you in this life. You can also use decrees to support this process, such as: "I AM the Violet Flame, transmuting all karmic patterns of illness and disease. I release these energies from my soul and body, freeing myself from all karmic ties."

For those who feel guided to incorporate other healing modalities into their Violet Flame practice, working with crystals can greatly enhance the healing process. Amethyst, with its deep connection to the Violet Flame, is a powerful stone for transmuting negative energy and promoting physical healing. You can place amethyst on the area of your body affected by illness during your meditations, or simply hold it in your hand as you work with the Violet Flame. Other helpful stones for healing chronic illness include rose quartz for emotional healing, clear quartz for amplifying energy, and black tourmaline for grounding and protection.

Herbs and essential oils can also be incorporated into your Violet Flame healing practice to support the body's physical healing. Essential oils such as lavender, frankincense, and eucalyptus have soothing, anti-inflammatory properties that can ease pain and discomfort while enhancing the energy work you are doing. You can apply these oils topically or diffuse them in your healing space, allowing their calming energy to assist in the healing process. Combining the physical healing properties of herbs and oils with the spiritual power of the Violet Flame creates a holistic approach that addresses all layers of the illness.

For more complex or severe chronic conditions, it may be helpful to engage in group healing or to work with a trained energy healer who can assist you in amplifying the power of the Violet Flame. Group healing sessions, in which several people focus their intention and energy on healing a specific individual or issue, can create a powerful vortex of healing energy that accelerates the process. If you feel drawn to this, consider joining a spiritual community or healing circle where you can share your journey and receive support from others who are also working with the Violet Flame.

Finally, it is essential to cultivate a mindset of patience and trust during your healing journey. Chronic illnesses often take time to heal, as they involve deep-rooted patterns that require sustained attention and energy work. Trust that each time you work with the Violet Flame, healing is occurring on multiple levels, even if the physical symptoms take time to shift. As you remain committed to your daily practice, allow yourself to rest in the knowledge that the healing process is unfolding in divine timing, and that you are supported every step of the way by the loving presence of Saint Germain and the Violet Flame.

In conclusion, the use of the Violet Flame for healing chronic illness is a powerful and transformative process that works on the physical, emotional, mental, and karmic levels. By incorporating daily rituals, meditative practices, decrees, and other healing modalities into your practice, you can create a holistic healing approach that addresses the root causes of illness and promotes lasting transformation. Through patience, dedication, and trust in the divine healing process, you can experience profound shifts in your health and well-being, opening the door to a life of greater balance, vitality, and spiritual alignment.

Chapter 23
Healing Animals with the Violet Flame

Animals, like humans, are energetic beings who respond to the vibrations of their environment. Their energy fields are sensitive to the emotions, thoughts, and energies of those around them. Just as humans can benefit from the healing power of the Violet Flame, so too can animals. Whether you are working with pets or other animals, the Violet Flame can assist in addressing their physical ailments, emotional traumas, or even behavioral issues that may stem from energetic imbalances.

Animals often experience the effects of energetic imbalances more acutely than humans, as they are more instinctively attuned to the energies surrounding them. Their natural sensitivity can make them more vulnerable to absorbing negative energy from their environment or their caretakers. If an animal is living in a stressful home environment, for example, it may take on the emotional energy of its owner, which can manifest as physical symptoms or changes in behavior. Similarly, animals that have experienced trauma—such as abuse, neglect, or abandonment—may carry lingering energetic wounds that impact their well-being.

The Violet Flame is uniquely suited to helping animals release these energetic blockages, as it works gently yet powerfully to transmute dense or negative energies and restore balance to the energy field. The healing process with animals often requires a deep sense of empathy and intuition, as they cannot verbally express their needs. By working with the Violet Flame, you can tune into the animal's energy, offering healing that reaches beyond the physical body and into the emotional and spiritual levels.

To begin using the Violet Flame for animal healing, it is important to first establish a connection with the animal's energy. Animals are highly intuitive, and they will often respond to your intentions and the energy you project toward them. Before starting the healing process, take a few moments to center yourself and create a space of calm and peace. This will help the animal feel safe and open to receiving the healing energy.

Prepare the Space: If possible, find a quiet and comfortable space where the animal can relax. You may want to light a candle or place calming crystals, such as rose quartz or amethyst, in the space to help create a soothing environment. If the animal is anxious or resistant to being in a specific space, allow it to choose where it feels most comfortable.

Ground and Center: Before you begin, take a few deep breaths to center yourself. Close your eyes and imagine roots extending from the soles of your feet into the Earth, grounding you. As you breathe, visualize yourself surrounded by the Violet Flame, clearing your energy and preparing you to act as a pure channel for healing.

Connect with the Animal's Energy: Gently place your hands near or on the animal, if it is comfortable with touch. If the animal is not receptive to physical contact, you can also work from a short distance by directing your energy toward them. As you connect with the animal's energy, set the intention to offer healing through the Violet Flame. Silently communicate to the animal that it is safe, loved, and supported, and that you are there to assist in its healing process.

Visualize the Violet Flame: Begin by visualizing the Violet Flame surrounding the animal, enveloping it in a gentle, protective light. Imagine the flame moving through the animal's body, dissolving any dense or stagnant energy that may be causing discomfort or illness. Focus on any areas of the animal's body that you sense are in need of healing. For example, if the animal has a specific injury or ailment, visualize the Violet Flame flowing directly into that area, burning away any negative energy and replacing it with vibrant, healing light.

Use Decrees for Healing: As you visualize the Violet Flame working through the animal's body, you can also use healing decrees to amplify the energy. Speak these decrees aloud or silently in your mind, directing them toward the animal. Some examples of decrees for animal healing include:

"I AM the Violet Flame, healing and restoring balance to [animal's name]."

"I command the Violet Flame to transmute all pain, fear, and imbalance from [animal's name]."

"I call upon the Violet Flame to restore divine health and vitality to [animal's name]."

As you repeat these decrees, feel the energy of the Violet Flame intensifying, working through all layers of the animal's being—physical, emotional, mental, and spiritual.

Observe the Animal's Response: Throughout the healing session, pay close attention to the animal's reactions. Some animals may become very relaxed, even falling asleep during the session, while others may become more energized or show signs of release, such as shaking, yawning, or stretching. These are all positive signs that the energy is moving and that the healing process is taking effect. If the animal becomes agitated or restless, this may indicate that too much energy is being introduced at once. In this case, gently ease back the intensity of the energy and allow the animal to integrate the healing at its own pace.

Close the Session with Gratitude: Once you feel that the healing session is complete, take a moment to express gratitude to the Violet Flame, to the animal, and to yourself for participating in the healing process. You might say: "Thank you, Violet Flame, for bringing healing and balance to [animal's name]. I trust that this healing will continue to unfold in perfect timing." Offer a final visualization of the Violet Flame surrounding the animal, sealing in the healing energy and providing ongoing protection.

Working with the Violet Flame on animals is often a subtle but deeply transformative process. In many cases, you may notice immediate shifts in the animal's energy or behavior, such as increased relaxation, improved mood, or relief from pain. In other instances, the effects may unfold gradually over time, especially if the animal is healing from long-term trauma or chronic conditions.

In addition to physical healing, the Violet Flame can also assist in emotional healing for animals that have experienced trauma, neglect, or abuse. Animals, like humans, can carry emotional wounds that manifest as anxiety, fear, aggression, or depression. These emotional wounds can be deeply ingrained, especially in animals that have been rescued or have had unstable lives. By using the Violet Flame, you can help these animals release the emotional baggage that they may be holding onto, allowing them to feel safe, loved, and at peace.

When working with emotionally traumatized animals, it is important to be especially patient and gentle. Some animals may be hesitant to receive healing energy at first, especially if they have been conditioned to distrust humans. In these cases, start by simply offering the energy from a distance, allowing the animal to choose whether to engage with it. Over time, as the animal begins to feel the safety and warmth of the healing energy, it will become more receptive to deeper healing.

For animals that are particularly anxious or fearful, you can also create an energetic shield using the Violet Flame to help them feel protected. Visualize the Violet Flame forming a bubble of light around the animal, creating a safe space where no harmful or negative energies can enter. This protective shield can help the animal feel more secure in its environment, especially if it is dealing with ongoing stress or anxiety.

Another way to support animals with the Violet Flame is by using crystals in combination with the energy work. Amethyst, in particular, is a powerful stone for healing animals, as it resonates with the energy of the Violet Flame and offers soothing, calming vibrations. You can place amethyst near the animal's bed or in the area where it spends the most time to create a continuous flow of healing energy. Other stones, such as rose quartz for emotional healing and clear quartz for amplifying energy, can also be beneficial when used in conjunction with the Violet Flame.

In summary, the Violet Flame is a powerful and compassionate tool for healing animals, addressing not only their physical ailments but also the emotional and energetic imbalances that may be affecting their well-being. Through visualization, decrees, and the gentle guidance of Saint Germain, you can offer profound healing to the animals in your care, helping them to release pain, trauma, and negativity, and to restore balance and harmony to their energy fields. As you continue to work with the Violet Flame for animal healing, you will develop a deeper understanding of the sacred bond between humans and animals and the incredible potential for healing that exists within this connection.

In the previous chapter, we explored how to establish a connection with animals and apply the Violet Flame for physical and emotional healing. Now, we will delve into specific techniques for working with the Violet Flame to address particular conditions and situations, including distance healing, healing of trauma, and creating energetic protection for pets. We will also discuss how to integrate other spiritual practices, such as invocations and prayers, into your healing work with animals to deepen the impact and bring lasting results.

One of the most powerful tools available when working with animals, especially those who may not be physically present, is distance healing. Animals, like humans, can receive healing energy no matter where they are located, as energy transcends time and space. This is particularly useful if you are working with an animal that is far away, in a shelter, or in a situation where direct contact is not possible. Distance healing can be just as effective as in-person healing and allows the animal to receive energy in its own space and on its own terms.

To begin a distance healing session for an animal, follow these steps:

Create a Sacred Space: Even though the animal is not physically present, it is important to prepare your space as if it were. Light a candle, place crystals around you (such as amethyst or clear quartz), and create a calm environment where you can focus on the healing process without distraction.

Visualize the Animal: Close your eyes and bring the image of the animal into your mind's eye. If you have a photograph of the animal, you can hold it in your hands to strengthen the connection. As you focus on the image, visualize the animal surrounded by the Violet Flame, gently purifying its energy field. Imagine the Violet Flame moving through the animal's body, transmuting any negative or stagnant energy and filling it with light.

Set the Intention for Healing: Silently or aloud, set the intention for the animal's healing. You might say: "I call upon the Violet Flame and the energy of Saint Germain to bring healing, peace, and protection to [animal's name]. May this healing energy flow to them now, wherever they are, transmuting all imbalances and restoring perfect health and harmony." As you set this intention, feel the energy of the Violet Flame expanding and moving toward the animal, connecting with it energetically.

Use Decrees: As with in-person healing, using decrees can amplify the energy of the Violet Flame in a distance healing session. Some examples of decrees you can use include:

"I AM the Violet Flame, surrounding [animal's name] in divine healing light."

"I command the Violet Flame to transmute all pain, fear, and imbalance from [animal's name] and restore their energy to perfect health."

"I call upon the Violet Flame to bring peace and healing to [animal's name], dissolving all negative energy and restoring balance."

Repeat these decrees as you visualize the energy moving through the animal's body, bringing healing to all levels of their being.

Release the Energy: Once you feel that the session is complete, thank the Violet Flame and Saint Germain for their assistance in the healing process. You might say: "Thank you,

Violet Flame, for bringing healing and balance to [animal's name]. I trust that this energy will continue to work in divine timing." Gently release the image of the animal, knowing that the energy will continue to flow to them as needed.

Trust in the Process: As with any form of energy healing, it is important to trust that the energy has reached the animal, even if you do not see immediate results. Animals often respond to healing energy in subtle ways, and the effects may unfold over time. Trust that the Violet Flame is working on the deepest levels of the animal's energy field, bringing balance and restoration where it is most needed.

In addition to distance healing, the Violet Flame is particularly effective in helping animals heal from trauma. Many animals, especially those that have been rescued from abusive or neglectful situations, carry deep emotional scars that may manifest as anxiety, fear, or aggression. These emotional wounds can be challenging to address, as animals are often unable to express their feelings verbally. However, the Violet Flame can gently transmute the emotional energy associated with trauma, helping animals release fear and heal on a deep spiritual level.

When working with animals that have experienced trauma, it is important to approach the healing process with great care and patience. Start by creating a space of safety and trust for the animal, allowing them to approach the healing energy at their own pace. Some animals may be hesitant to receive healing energy at first, especially if they have been conditioned to fear humans. In these cases, it is helpful to begin by simply offering the energy from a distance, as discussed earlier. Over time, as the animal begins to feel the calming presence of the Violet Flame, they will become more open to receiving deeper healing.

For animals dealing with emotional trauma, you can also use the Violet Flame to clear cords and attachments that may be contributing to their distress. These cords may be connected to past owners, traumatic experiences, or even energetic imprints left behind by other animals. To do this, visualize the Violet Flame cutting through any cords or attachments that are draining the animal's energy or causing them emotional pain. As you do this, use decrees such as:

"I AM the Violet Flame, dissolving all cords and attachments from [animal's name] that no longer serve their highest good."

"I command the Violet Flame to transmute all trauma, fear, and emotional pain from [animal's name] and restore them to perfect peace and harmony."

As the cords are released, visualize the Violet Flame sealing any remaining energetic wounds, filling them with light and love.

Protection is another essential aspect of working with animals, particularly for pets or animals that are regularly exposed to stressful environments. Just as humans can benefit from energetic protection, animals also need to be shielded from negative influences that may impact their well-being. This is especially true for sensitive animals, such as cats or dogs, who are highly attuned to the emotions and energies of their human companions.

You can create an energetic shield for animals using the Violet Flame, offering them ongoing protection from harmful energies. To do this, visualize the Violet Flame forming a protective bubble of light around the animal, creating a shield that deflects any negative or harmful energies. You can also use crystals such as black tourmaline or smoky quartz to strengthen this protection, placing them near the animal's bed or in areas where they spend a lot of time. As you create this shield, use decrees such as:

"I AM the Violet Flame, surrounding [animal's name] in divine protection."

"I call upon the Violet Flame to create a shield of light around [animal's name], protecting them from all harm and negativity."

This energetic shield can be reinforced regularly, particularly if the animal is exposed to stressful situations or environments. For example, if your pet becomes anxious during car rides, vet visits, or when strangers are around, you can visualize the Violet Flame protecting them during these moments, helping them to feel safe and secure.

In situations where an animal is nearing the end of its life, the Violet Flame can also assist in providing comfort and spiritual support during the transition process. Animals, like humans, often experience anxiety or fear as they prepare to cross over, and the Violet Flame can help ease these emotions by surrounding the animal with a sense of peace and light. During this time, you can work with the Violet Flame to create a peaceful and loving environment for the animal, offering them reassurance and support as they transition.

To assist an animal during this process, visualize the Violet Flame enveloping them in a cocoon of light, gently dissolving any fear or pain they may be experiencing. As you do this, use decrees such as:

"I AM the Violet Flame, surrounding [animal's name] with love, peace, and comfort as they transition to the next phase of their journey."

"I call upon the Violet Flame to bring healing and release to [animal's name], allowing them to pass peacefully and with grace."

In conclusion, the Violet Flame offers a powerful and compassionate tool for healing animals, whether they are experiencing physical illness, emotional trauma, or energetic imbalances. Through distance healing, trauma release, and energetic protection, you can support the animals in your care with love and light, helping them to find peace, health, and harmony. As you continue to work with the Violet Flame in your healing practice, you will deepen your connection with the animal kingdom and play an important role in their spiritual well-being.

Chapter 24
Advancing in Global and Planetary Healing

As we move beyond personal and localized healing, the teachings of Saint Germain and the Violet Flame extend into a much broader context: global and planetary healing. The interconnectedness of all life on Earth means that the energy of individual healing naturally ripples out to affect the larger collective. Likewise, the health of the planet, its ecosystems, and its inhabitants are intimately linked. Global healing, therefore, requires a holistic approach that not only heals individuals but also works to restore balance to the Earth and its energy grid.

At this critical time in human history, the Earth is undergoing a profound energetic transformation. Many believe that this transformation is part of the spiritual awakening of humanity, a shift into higher consciousness that involves the raising of the planet's vibrational frequency. However, this shift also brings challenges, including environmental degradation, social unrest, and collective energetic imbalances. To address these issues, Saint Germain's teachings emphasize the importance of lightworkers and healers engaging in planetary healing work. By invoking the Violet Flame and participating in global healing rituals, you can contribute to the restoration of the Earth's energy and help elevate the vibration of the entire planet.

Planetary healing begins with an understanding that the Earth itself is a living, breathing being with its own energy field, often referred to as the planetary grid or ley lines. Just as humans have chakras and energy centers, the Earth has its own network of energy points that carry vital spiritual energy throughout the planet. Over time, negative human actions—such as pollution, deforestation, and conflict—have created blockages in this grid, contributing to environmental destruction and energetic stagnation. The Violet Flame is a powerful tool for transmuting these dense energies, clearing the planetary grid, and restoring the natural flow of divine energy.

To engage in global and planetary healing, it is important to first attune your personal energy to the higher frequencies required for this work. This attunement can be achieved through regular meditation, invocation of the Violet Flame, and practices that raise your own vibrational frequency, such as acts of compassion, gratitude, and service to others. By maintaining a high vibration, you can act as a clearer channel for the healing energy needed to assist the planet.

A practical way to participate in planetary healing is by engaging in group meditations or collective rituals focused on global transformation. When individuals come together with the shared intention of healing the planet, their combined energy creates a powerful vortex that can significantly amplify the healing process. You can join or organize meditation groups that focus on using the Violet Flame to transmute negative energy from the Earth and to send healing light to areas of the planet in need of restoration.

To begin, here is a suggested meditation for planetary healing with the Violet Flame:

Create Sacred Space: As with any healing work, it is important to prepare your space before starting. Light a candle, burn incense, or place crystals such as amethyst or clear quartz around you to create a peaceful atmosphere. If you are working with a group, ensure that everyone is seated in a comfortable and calm environment, ready to focus their energy on the Earth.

Center and Ground Yourself: Take several deep breaths, inhaling through your nose and exhaling through your mouth. With each breath, feel your body relaxing and your mind becoming more focused. Visualize roots extending from the soles of your feet into the Earth, grounding you in its energy. Allow yourself to become fully present in the moment.

Invoke the Violet Flame: Silently or aloud, call upon the Violet Flame and Saint Germain to assist in this planetary healing meditation. You might say: "I call upon the Violet Flame and the energy of Saint Germain to assist in the healing of the Earth. May the Violet Flame transmute all dense and negative energies from the planet and restore the flow of divine light throughout the Earth's energy grid."

Visualize the Earth Surrounded by the Violet Flame: As you close your eyes, bring an image of the Earth into your mind's eye. See the planet surrounded by the soft, purifying light of the Violet Flame. Visualize the flame moving through the Earth's energy grid, dissolving blockages, pollution, and negativity. As the Violet Flame travels through the planet's ley lines, imagine it restoring balance and harmony to all corners of the Earth.

Focus on Areas in Need of Healing: Once you have visualized the Earth as a whole, focus your attention on specific areas of the planet that are in need of healing. This could include regions affected by war, natural disasters, environmental destruction, or social unrest. As you visualize these areas, send the Violet Flame directly to them, imagining the energy clearing away all negative influences and restoring peace and harmony. You might repeat decrees such as:

"I AM the Violet Flame, healing and restoring peace to [name of area]."

"I command the Violet Flame to transmute all negativity and suffering from [name of area] and replace it with divine light."

Send Healing to the Earth's Elements: In addition to focusing on specific regions, you can also direct healing energy toward the elements of the Earth—air, water, fire, and earth. Visualize the Violet Flame purifying the air we breathe, clearing away pollution and toxins. See it moving through the oceans, rivers, and lakes, transmuting pollutants and restoring the purity of the planet's waters. Imagine the flame moving through the soil, healing the Earth and renewing its vitality. Finally, visualize the Violet Flame working through the fire element, bringing balance to areas experiencing wildfires or excessive heat.

Anchor the Healing Energy: Once you have completed the visualization, imagine the Violet Flame anchoring itself into the Earth's core, creating a permanent flow of divine energy that continues to heal the planet even after the meditation ends. You might say: "I anchor the Violet Flame into the heart of the Earth, allowing its energy to continue healing and restoring balance to the planet."

Express Gratitude: Take a few moments to thank the Violet Flame, Saint Germain, and any other spiritual beings you have called upon for their assistance in this healing work. Feel a deep sense of gratitude for the healing that has taken place, both for the planet and for yourself as a participant in this global transformation.

Collective rituals are another powerful way to engage in planetary healing. These rituals can be performed with a group of like-minded individuals, either in person or virtually, with the shared intention of invoking the Violet Flame to assist in global transformation. During these rituals, participants can focus their energy on specific global issues, such as environmental crises, social justice movements, or the healing of human consciousness. By uniting in this way, the collective energy generated can create a profound ripple effect, influencing the collective consciousness and contributing to global healing.

In addition to meditations and rituals, you can contribute to planetary healing by engaging in acts of service that benefit the Earth and its inhabitants. This could include participating in environmental conservation efforts, supporting organizations that work toward social and environmental justice, or simply living in a way that honors and respects the planet. Every small action taken to reduce your ecological footprint, protect wildlife, or promote peace contributes to the overall healing of the Earth.

It is also important to acknowledge that planetary healing requires the healing of human consciousness. Many of the challenges facing the Earth today—such as pollution, climate change, and deforestation—are the result of human actions and imbalances in collective consciousness. As individuals, we are each responsible for healing the aspects of ourselves that contribute to these imbalances, whether they are patterns of fear, greed, or separation. By using the Violet Flame to heal our own consciousness and align ourselves with higher spiritual principles, we can contribute to the elevation of the collective consciousness and create a more harmonious relationship with the Earth.

As a lightworker, your role in planetary healing is not just limited to your own healing work but also involves inspiring and guiding others to participate in this global transformation. You can share the teachings of the Violet Flame with those around you, encouraging them to engage in their own healing practices and to contribute to the collective effort of raising the vibration of the planet. Through your example, you can help others see the importance of working together to heal the Earth and to create a world that is aligned with the principles of love, compassion, and spiritual growth.

The work of global and planetary healing is essential for the future of the Earth and humanity. Through the Violet Flame, you have access to a powerful tool that can transmute the dense energies affecting the planet, restore balance to the Earth's energy grid, and elevate the vibration of human consciousness. By participating in collective meditations, rituals, and acts of service, you can contribute to this profound transformation and play an important role in the healing of the planet. As you continue your work as a healer and lightworker, remember that every act of healing, no matter how small, contributes to the greater whole and brings us closer to a world of peace, harmony, and spiritual awakening.

In this final chapter, we deepen our exploration of global and planetary healing with the Violet Flame, focusing on collective rituals, meditations, and understanding the role of lightworkers in transforming Earth's energy field. The work of Saint Germain is not only about individual healing but also about healing the collective consciousness and the planet as a whole. With the challenges that humanity faces—ranging from environmental destruction to social and political unrest—this healing work is more vital than ever.

The Violet Flame, as a tool of spiritual alchemy, plays a crucial role in transmuting negative energies, whether they are personal, societal, or planetary. Its unique ability to dissolve low-vibrational patterns allows it to be directed toward large-scale healing efforts, making it a powerful force for planetary transformation. As lightworkers, we are called to participate in this process, not only by working on our personal growth but by directing our efforts toward global healing.

A key aspect of advancing in planetary healing is to understand the collective consciousness. Collective consciousness refers to the shared beliefs, thoughts, and emotions of humanity that shape global events and the state of the world. Over time, negative patterns in the collective consciousness, such as fear, anger, and division, have contributed to the imbalance and suffering we see on the planet. By using the Violet Flame, lightworkers can help transmute these dense energies and replace them with the higher vibrations of love, peace, and unity.

Group rituals and meditations are particularly effective in amplifying the energy of the Violet Flame. When multiple people focus their intentions on healing the Earth and humanity, the combined energy creates a powerful wave of transformation that can have far-reaching effects. Whether you are joining a group in person or participating in a virtual meditation, the collective focus on healing accelerates the process and brings greater light to the planet.

One of the most potent rituals for planetary healing involves anchoring the Violet Flame in key locations around the world. These locations may include places of environmental degradation, areas affected by conflict or natural disasters, or specific energetic points on the Earth's grid, such as sacred sites or ley lines. By anchoring the Violet Flame in these locations, you can create lasting energetic shifts that support the healing and restoration of the planet.

To anchor the Violet Flame in a specific location, follow this ritual:

Prepare Your Space: Begin by creating a sacred space where you can focus on the planetary healing work. Light a candle, burn incense, or use crystals such as amethyst or clear quartz to enhance the energy. If you are working with a group, gather in a circle and take a few moments to center yourselves.

Ground Yourself: Take several deep breaths to ground and center your energy. Visualize roots extending from your feet into the Earth, connecting you with the planet's energy. Feel the grounding and stabilizing force of the Earth beneath you, anchoring you in the present moment.

Invoke the Violet Flame: Call upon the Violet Flame and Saint Germain to assist in the planetary healing work. You might say: "I call upon the Violet Flame and the energy of Saint Germain to assist in the healing of the Earth. May the Violet Flame be anchored in [specific location], transmuting all negative energy and restoring balance and harmony."

Visualize the Location: Bring the image of the specific location you are focusing on into your mind's eye. This could be a region affected by war, a polluted area, or a sacred site that needs energetic restoration. As you visualize the location, see the Violet Flame descending from the spiritual realms and enveloping the area in a powerful, purifying light.

Anchor the Violet Flame: As you hold the vision of the Violet Flame surrounding the location, imagine it penetrating deep into the Earth, anchoring itself into the planet's core. Visualize the Violet Flame dissolving all negative energy, transmuting fear, anger, and pain into light. See the energy spreading throughout the surrounding region, uplifting the vibration of the land, the people, and the Earth itself.

Use Decrees to Amplify the Energy: To strengthen the anchoring process, use powerful decrees that focus on planetary healing. Some examples include:

"I AM the Violet Flame, transmuting all negativity in [specific location] and restoring divine harmony."

"I command the Violet Flame to anchor in [specific location], dissolving all fear, conflict, and suffering, and replacing it with peace and light."

"I call upon the Violet Flame to uplift the vibration of the Earth and all its inhabitants, bringing healing to every corner of the planet."

Repeat these decrees as you visualize the Violet Flame continuing to flow through the location, purifying and restoring balance.

Expand the Healing Energy: Once the Violet Flame has been anchored in the location, expand your focus to include the entire planet. Visualize the Violet Flame surrounding the Earth, transmuting all dense and negative energies from the collective consciousness. See the flame moving through the Earth's energy grid, restoring the flow of divine light and uplifting the vibration of the entire planet.

Seal the Healing with Gratitude: When you feel the ritual is complete, take a moment to express gratitude to the Violet Flame, Saint Germain, and any other spiritual beings you have called upon for their assistance. You might say: "Thank you, Violet Flame, for bringing healing, peace, and balance to the Earth. I trust that this energy will continue to work for the highest good of all."

Group meditations that focus on global healing are another powerful way to advance in planetary transformation. These meditations can be organized around significant global events, full moons, equinoxes, or other energetic portals when the collective energy is especially potent. During these times, lightworkers around the world can join together in meditation to send the Violet Flame to areas in need, collectively amplifying the healing energy.

A simple group meditation for global healing with the Violet Flame could follow this structure:

Opening the Circle: Begin by creating a circle of light with your group, whether in person or virtually. You can visualize a circle of Violet Flame surrounding the group, connecting each participant with the energy of healing and transformation.

Invocation: Together, invoke the presence of Saint Germain and the Violet Flame. You might say: "We call upon the Violet Flame and the energy of Saint Germain to assist in the healing of the Earth and the upliftment of humanity. May the Violet Flame transmute all negativity from the planet and restore divine harmony."

Visualization: Each participant visualizes the Earth surrounded by the Violet Flame, with the flame moving through the planet's energy grid. Focus on sending healing energy to specific regions of the world in need of peace, restoration, and balance. As you visualize the Violet Flame moving through the planet, feel its energy growing stronger with each participant's contribution.

Decrees: Use collective decrees to amplify the energy. The group can repeat these decrees together, creating a powerful vibration of healing that resonates with the planet. For example:

"We are the Violet Flame, bringing healing and peace to the Earth."

"We command the Violet Flame to transmute all suffering, fear, and negativity from the collective consciousness."

"We anchor the Violet Flame in the heart of the Earth, restoring balance and harmony to all beings."

Closing the Meditation: Once the meditation is complete, close the circle by offering gratitude to the Violet Flame, Saint Germain, and the spiritual forces of light that have assisted in the healing process. Trust that the energy generated in the meditation will continue to ripple out, contributing to global transformation.

As you continue your work in global and planetary healing, it is important to understand the role of the lightworker. Lightworkers are spiritual pioneers who bring higher frequencies of light into the physical world, helping to elevate the consciousness of humanity and the Earth. By working with the Violet Flame, you are not only healing yourself and others but also assisting in the great shift that is taking place on the planet.

The role of a lightworker extends beyond personal spiritual practice. It involves living in alignment with higher principles of love, compassion, and service. Lightworkers are called to lead by example, inspiring others through their actions and their commitment to healing the Earth. Whether through environmental activism, humanitarian efforts, or simply spreading love and kindness in everyday interactions, lightworkers play a crucial role in the transformation of the world.

Planetary healing is not an isolated practice but part of a larger spiritual evolution that is unfolding on Earth. As the vibration of the planet rises, more and more individuals are awakening to their role as healers and lightworkers, joining together in a collective effort to create a world of peace, harmony, and unity. By continuing to work with the Violet Flame and participating in global healing rituals, you are contributing to this evolution and helping to usher in a new era of spiritual awakening.

In conclusion, the work of global and planetary healing is a profound and essential aspect of the teachings of Saint Germain and the Violet Flame. Through collective rituals, meditations, and the anchoring of light in key locations, lightworkers can assist in the transformation of the Earth and the elevation of human consciousness. As you continue on your path as a lightworker, remember that every act of healing contributes to the greater whole, bringing us closer to a world of peace, love, and spiritual enlightenment.

Epilogue

As you reach the end of this journey, you must have realized that the process of healing goes far beyond the physical body. What began as a quest for balance and well-being has revealed itself as a profound reconnection with your own divinity. Now, as you close these pages, a new chapter of your life begins—a chapter you will write with a renewed understanding of energy, healing, and, above all, of yourself.

The flames that accompanied you on this journey—especially the Violet Flame—are not just spiritual tools but portals to higher levels of consciousness. In working with these energies, you have learned that true healing is not merely physical but an inner alchemy that transforms old patterns, emotions, and karmic wounds into light, love, and peace. You have awakened to the fact that every healing process is, in truth, a soul's liberation.

You were invited to explore powerful practices of meditation, visualization, and decrees that connect your energy to universal forces of transformation. Now, it's time to reflect on how much you have grown. You began this journey with questions, doubts, and perhaps deep wounds. But as each page unfolded, something inside you began to shift. The weight you carried gave way to a newfound lightness, and uncertainty was replaced with clarity and purpose.

But the path of healing is infinite. The flames you have awakened will continue to guide you. This journey does not end here; this is merely the beginning of a life where you can apply these healing techniques daily—not just for yourself but for the world around you. With each practice, with each connection to higher energies, you will strengthen the light that already shines within.

Remember that the energies you encountered are not passive. They are alive, active, and ready to manifest whenever you call upon them. The true wisdom this book revealed is that you are the agent of your own transformation. The power of healing does not lie outside of you but within, waiting to be channeled, directed, and manifested in every area of your life.

Now that you know the secrets of holistic healing, what else can you achieve? What else can you transform into light? The possibilities are limitless. The sacred flames continue to burn, and whenever you feel the need to renew your strength, you can invoke them—no matter where you are, their power is just a thought away.

This book was only an introduction to wisdom that transcends time. Daily practice and deeper immersion in the knowledge it offers will open doors to an even greater level of healing and spiritual evolution. But above all, it has empowered you to take ownership of your own journey. You now possess the tools and knowledge not only to heal but to guide others along the same path.

So, as the final words of this work resonate in your mind, remember that your journey continues. The power of the sacred flames has no end, just as your capacity to grow and evolve spiritually has no limits. You have emerged from this experience with something that no one can take away from you: the knowledge that you are a channel of light and healing. And with this knowledge, you can not only transform your life but also the world around you.

May the flames continue to illuminate your path. May love, healing, and transformation be your constant companions. And may you continue to be a beacon of light for those who seek their own healing, just as you have sought yours.

Milton Keynes UK
Ingram Content Group UK Ltd.
UKHW042244011124
450424UK00001BA/224